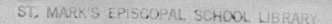

DISCOVER CANADA

Nova Scotia

By Jim Lotz

Consultants

Desmond Morton, FRSC, Professor of History, University of Toronto

Peter Kidd, M.A., Learning Materials Consulting Services, Halifax

Grolier Limited
TORONTO

Minas Basin farmland at low tide
Overleaf: **Rocky bay along the coast of Cape Breton Island**

Canadian Cataloguing in Publication Data

Lotz, Jim, 1929-
  Nova Scotia

(Discover Canada)
Rev. ed.
Includes index.
ISBN 0-7172-3140-2

1. Nova Scotia — Juvenile literature. I. Title.
II. Series: Discover Canada (Toronto, Ont.).

FC2311.2.L67 1996   j971.6   C96-931031-5
F1037.4.L67 1996

Front cover: Aerial view of the Halifax Waterfront
Back cover: Cabot Trail, Cape Breton Highlands
National Park, Cape Breton Island

Printed and bound in Canada.
Published simultaneously in the United States.
  3 4 5 6 7 8 9 10 DWF 99 98 97 96

Row houses in Halifax

Table of Contents

CHAPTER 1

Nova Scotia: Almost an Island

Shaped like a lobster, Nova Scotia hangs on to Canada by a narrow strip of land. Only the Isthmus of Chignecto, 26 kilometres (16 miles) wide, prevents the province from being an island. No Nova Scotian lives more than an hour's drive from the coast.

The province is small but amazingly varied. Handsome houses line the streets of towns where time seems almost to have stopped. Nearby, modern shopping malls lure customers to their brightly lit stores. Almost within hearing range, endless Atlantic waves crash on barren shores where fishing villages cling to the coasts. Everywhere lies evidence of sieges, shipwrecks, long-vanished ways of life. From North America's first tidal power plant you can see the site of Canada's first European settlement.

The people of Nova Scotia are as varied as the scenery. It was not always so. Once, the native Micmac had the land to themselves and used its resources to create a strong culture. Almost four hundred years ago, they were joined by the first European settlers, the French-speaking Acadians, and later by Loyalists fleeing from the new-born republic to the south and by Scots thrown off their small highland farms to make way for sheep. Today, people from all over the world live and work in the province.

Making a living in Nova Scotia was never easy. Its people learned to farm barren land, build strong ships, sail through storms and raise sturdy families. They learned to change — and to endure.

Nova Scotia today faces the future with some uncertainty. As they are drawn into an increasingly competitive world economy, Nova Scotians can learn much from those who went before them and created a unique lifestyle on the sea-washed shores of this enchanting part of Canada.

Yarmouth Light. The beam from this historic light can be seen almost 50 km (30 mi.) out to sea.

CHAPTER 2

The Land

W

ith an area of 55 491 square kilometres (21 420 square miles), Nova Scotia is the second-smallest province in Canada. The Atlantic Ocean washes the eastern shores of the province. Northumberland Strait separates it from Prince Edward Island. To the northwest, the Nova Scotia coast faces New Brunswick across the Bay of Fundy.

The Shape of the Land

Rolling hills dominate the landscape of Nova Scotia. They are the remains of ancient mountains worn down to mere stubs by glaciers and weather. The province has five different upland areas. The Southern Uplands cover most of south and central Nova Scotia. The North Mountain runs along the Bay of Fundy between it and the Annapolis Valley. The Cobequid Mountains lie to the northwest, and to the east, the Pictou and Antigonish highlands and the Cape Breton highlands dominate the landscape. None of these upland areas rise above 573 metres (1880 feet), but many spectacular cliffs, like Cape Smoky and Cape Blomidon, tower above the sea.

Brick-red and white cliffs appear where sandstone and limestone underlie the land. Ancient seas left deposits of salt at Pugwash and of gypsum near Little Narrows and Hantsport. Centuries of dead forests formed the deposits of coal in Cape Breton, Pictou and Cumberland counties. As the ice retreated from Nova Scotia about 12 000 years ago, it scraped the land bare in some areas, dropped

Overleaf: In the rolling hills of Pictou County, Scottish settlers found land that reminded them of home.

The breathtaking
sandstone cliffs of
Cape Split overlook
the Minas Channel.

seas of boulders in others and deposited rich soil in scattered
places. Sir William Alexander, an early promoter of the province,
praised its "very delicate meadows, with roses white and red, and
the very good fat earth" in a book published in 1624. Very few
places in Nova Scotia fit this description, however, and only 10 percent of its surface can be farmed. Most of the flat and fertile land
lies along Northumberland Strait, around Minas Basin, and down
the Annapolis Valley.

Large parts of the province are dotted with small lakes connected
by slow-moving streams. The Shubenacadie-Stewiacke system is
the province's longest river. The Annapolis River wanders lazily
down the valley that bears its name. Near the coasts short, swift
streams rush to the sea.

The squid-shaped Bay of Fundy, lying between Nova Scotia and
New Brunswick, has the world's highest tides. They rise and fall by
as much as 17 metres (56 feet) as water is funnelled into the bay. As
the glaciers retreated, the seas rose, drowning low-lying land on
Cape Breton Island and creating the Bras d'Or lake system in its
centre. Open to the sea but with tides that are barely noticeable, the
lake is ideal for yachting.

Climate

Nova Scotia has a maritime climate. The seas around the province heat up slowly during the summer and cool off gradually during the fall. Winter arrives in early December and lasts until March, but night frosts can strike in low-lying areas and cold winds may blow down the streets of Halifax until late May. Mid-spring through to early summer is the season of fogs. Fall, with warm days and cool nights, is the most pleasant season of the Nova Scotia year.

Southwest Nova Scotia is frost-free for over half the year, but winter lingers long in the highlands of Cape Breton where subarctic vegetation flourishes. Average July afternoon temperatures seldom go above 25°C (77°F). January night-time lows usually hover around -10°C (14°F). As well as being cool, Nova Scotia is damp. Most of the province receives over 1000 millimetres (39 inches) of precipitation.

Nova Scotia has been described as "the stormiest region of Canada." Storms move across the province from the west or sweep up the east coast of the United States. In summer these storms drench the province with rain. In winter they dump snow and send skiers off to the slopes of Cape Smoky and the Wentworth Valley. One of the worst storms on record hit Cape Breton Island on August 25, 1873. The tail end of a hurricane took 500 lives, destroyed 1200 vessels and smashed 900 buildings into splinters.

Vegetation

Nova Scotia's moist climate produces a rich forest growth. Few stands of the original hardwood forests remain. Over much of the province hardwoods, such as oak and maple, have largely been replaced by coniferous trees, which thrive on acid soil and a cool climate. Today red spruce, balsam fir and pine dominate the forests. Enough hardwoods remain, however, to brighten the evergreen shades in the fall with their changing colours. Rosemary, bog-

Farmland outside the village of
Canning, near Cape Blomidon.
Inset: Winter at West Dover, on the
South Shore

laurel, tamarack and alder grow well on poorly drained land. In
many parts of the province, alder and pasture spruce have moved
onto abandoned farmland. Burned-over areas grow blueberries,
cherry, aspen and red maple. Mayflowers, wild iris, pitcher plant,
white water lilies, and violets flourish in Nova Scotia.

The operations of pulp and paper mills in the province in this
century have further altered the composition of the forests. The
mills use mainly softwood, so the growth of hardwoods is slowed
by spraying. Some efforts to conserve the softwood forests have
been controversial. In 1976, the spruce budworm, a forest pest,
was destroying many of the spruce trees in Cape Breton. The government allowed the trees to be sprayed from the air to kill the
budworm. Local people, concerned about the impact of spraying on
their health, protested. Two years later the province banned aerial
spraying. Many hills in Cape Breton turned white with trees killed
by the budworm. Fortunately, the destructive insect now appears to
be under control.

Sable Island, a narrow sandbar 285 km (185 mi.) east of Halifax, is famous for its wild horses. The herd, descended from domestic horses brought to the island about 250 years ago, ranges in size from 150 to 400 animals.

Animals and Birds

Animal and bird life has also been greatly altered by the presence of humans in the province. The Micmac lived lightly on the land, hunting caribou and moose and taking bear, beaver and muskrat for food and furs. Passenger pigeons darkened the skies as did other migratory birds such as plovers and doves, and residents like black ducks and puffins.

As European settlement spread, larger animals, like the moose, retreated further into the forests. Caribou disappeared entirely from the province. Skunks and porcupines are common, but not on Cape Breton. The marten, however, survives only on the island. Black bear, beaver, bobcat, chipmunk, otter and snowshoe hare are found throughout the province, and cougars roam isolated areas.

Gulls on the seawall at Glace Bay on Cape Breton Island. *Inset*: Great blue heron

Fast, cunning white-tailed deer can often be seen near highways. They were introduced into Nova Scotia in the 1920s for hunters. They browse where forests have been recently cut down, and on overgrown pastures and vacant farms. Caribou have been reintroduced in Cape Breton Highlands National Park and are thriving.

Other species of animal have arrived in the province, sometimes creating problems. No one is sure how raccoons reached Nova Scotia, but they annoy many people by raiding garbage cans for food. Perhaps the most troublesome new arrival is the coyote, which first appeared in 1977. Again, it is not known where they came from, but they have been causing problems for farmers by killing sheep.

The passenger pigeon is now extinct, but a vast assortment of birds still thrive in Nova Scotia. Over 200 species have been reported in the Tantramar marsh, which links Nova Scotia and New Brunswick. The mudflats around the Bay of Fundy come alive with sandpipers and other migratory birds in the spring and fall. The harsh cry of the blue jay is heard in the heart of Halifax and songbirds like the redstart, yellow goldfinch and black-capped chickadee call in rural areas. Bald eagles nest in remote locations, sweeping down their flyways in search of food. Great blue herons and double-crested cormorants wait patiently at tidal pools to catch unwary fish.

Countless species of fish and shellfish thrive in Nova Scotia coastal and inland waters. Whales in search of krill, the small creatures they feed on, frequent the coasts, especially in the Bay of Fundy. Large numbers of harbour and grey seals can be found around the coasts.

The Environment and Pollution

Wherever people live and work the natural environment is changed, often for the worse. While many parts of Nova Scotia remain almost untouched, industry and population growth have created serious pollution in others.

In Sydney, a plume of orange smoke rose from the steel plant and hung heavily over the city for years. Recent modernization of the mill has removed this source of pollution, and pulp and paper mills that polluted rivers and streams are also cleaning up their operations.

The Halifax-Dartmouth area has the province's largest concentration of people — and of garbage. Soon the local landfill site will be unable to take any more garbage. Re-use, recycling and composting are being promoted in many communities around the province as a way of protecting the environment.

Few Nova Scotian communities treat their sewage before it flows into the ocean or a river. Each day, 220 million litres (60 million gallons) of waste water pour into Halifax harbour. In 1990 the federal and provincial governments began to study ways of cleaning up the harbour. However the high cost of doing this resulted in plans for sewage treatment being cancelled, and the harbour remains polluted.

Some pollution comes from outside the province. Lakes and trees have been increasingly damaged by acid rain from sources in the industrial heart of North America. And dangerous seas and careless seamen have led to ocean pollution. In February 1970, the tanker *Arrow* hit a rock off the southeast coast of Cape Breton. The wreck dumped six million litres (1.6 million gallons) of oil into the sea, fouling the nearby shores. Icy waters, freezing temperatures, and gale force winds made it difficult to contain and collect the spilled oil. After this incident, stricter policies were enforced to control shipping and pollution around Canada's coasts.

Both the federal and the provincial governments are beginning to deal with environmental problems. They are encouraging development and growth that does as little harm as possible to the landscape, vegetation and wildlife of the province.

Salmon fishing on Cape Breton Island. Nova Scotians value their sparkling lakes and rivers and are doing all they can to preserve them. A major concern remains — ever higher levels of acid rain created by industries outside the province.

CHAPTER 3

Beginnings

When the last ice age ended, caribou and other wildlife moved into Nova Scotia, grazing on the vegetation that sprang up as the ground thawed. Behind them, about 10 600 years ago, came the earliest humans. Chipped-stone tools and stone weapons made by these people have been found at Debert, near Truro.

The earliest written records we have about Nova Scotia's native people date from the early seventeenth century. By then they had a well-developed culture. Known as "Micmac" from their word *nikmaq* which means "my kin folk," they made skilful use of the resources of land, sea and river. They moved with the changing seasons, rarely staying more than five or six weeks in one place. In spring they divided into small bands and moved to the seashore, where they collected shellfish and caught smelt, salmon and herring. Summer brought pigeons, partridges, hares and rabbits. In the fall and winter the Micmac hunted eels, seals, beaver, otter, bear, moose and caribou.

From the forest came tree bark for houses, canoes and containers, and wood for fires to smoke fish and meat. The land provided blueberries, raspberries and strawberries, roots for medicine, and fibres for making twine and rope.

In 1672, Nicolas Denys, a French explorer and trader, wrote sympathetically of the Micmac way of life. He told how they made clothing and bags from cedar bark, nettles, Indian hemp (a tough weed) and sweet grass, and decorated them with porcupine quills.

A recreation of Micmac life in the days before European settlement. At that time the Micmac occupied the Gaspé Peninsula as well as most of today's Maritime Provinces.

The Coming of the Europeans

There is evidence to suggest that Norsemen reached Nova Scotia a thousand years ago, and a Scottish nobleman, Henry Sinclair, Earl of Orkney, may have come to the province in 1398. It is certain, however, that Europeans arrived in the sixteenth century.

When John Cabot left Bristol in 1497, he hoped to reach China by sailing across the Atlantic. Instead, he landed on the shores of North America on June 24 and claimed the new-found land for King Henry VII and England. No one is sure where Cabot landed. Newfoundland's claim to be the site is probably the strongest. The people of Cape Breton, however, celebrate Cabot's arrival at Aspy Bay each year and the trail around the northern tip of the island is named after him.

Although Cabot did not find the riches of the Far East, he found some of the best fishing grounds in the world. The Labrador current sweeps around Newfoundland and meets the Gulf Stream coming from the south. The mixing of the waters off Newfoundland and Nova Scotia creates conditions in which cod and other fish thrive. Cabot returned to England with tales of seas alive with fish. And so began the "Cod Rush." Over the next hundred years, sailors from European ports set out to catch fish in Newfoundland and Nova Scotia waters. In the late 1570s an English merchant estimated that 400 Portuguese, Spanish, French and English ships fished these waters.

Some fish was salted and stored in barrels on the ships, but some was taken ashore and dried at fishing stations. In 1604 France set up a station at Canso. At first European fishermen were not interested in settling permanently on the shores of this new land. A French sea captain in 1607 said he was "wondrous content" with the fishery. His vessel had made forty-two voyages across the North Atlantic, returning each time with almost 50 000 kilograms (110 000 pounds) of dried fish. Why should anyone leave such a life and try to make a living on the desolate shores of Nova Scotia?

Micmac hunter. The Micmac and the French got along well from the beginning and soon became quite dependent on each other.

Nonetheless, trade slowly began between the native people and the fishermen. Native people wanted European goods — iron tools, copper kettles, cloth and blankets. The fishermen and explorers were interested in furs because the market for them in Europe was growing rapidly.

The First Settlements

In the great age of European expansion, explorers claimed the lands they "discovered" in the name of their kings and queens. It sometimes happened that the same land was claimed in the name of two — or even more — monarchs, who then gave grants to individuals to trade and settle in these lands.

At the beginning of the seventeenth century French attention focused on the area of the present-day Maritime provinces. In 1604, Pierre du Gua de Monts, a French nobleman, received the right to settle, trade and fish in the region. He established a settlement at

Every two weeks one member of the Order of Good Cheer took his turn at providing an evening's food and entertainment. Such an evening is re-enacted here at the reconstructed Port Royal Habitation.

the mouth of the St. Croix River in what is now New Brunswick. After a terrible winter during which many settlers died, the survivors moved to a sheltered, well-watered site they called Port Royal on the Annapolis Basin. Among their number was Samuel de Champlain, who later mapped New France and became its governor.

Champlain and his companions put up a fortress called the *habitation*. They also built a lime kiln, forge and grist mill, and planted vegetables and grain. To keep up morale, they established Canada's first social club — the Order of Good Cheer. Canada's first play, *Le Théâtre de Neptune*, was performed at Port Royal.

The French settlers learned much from the Micmac, with whom they established friendly relationships. Among other things, the native people taught them how to make birchbark canoes and snowshoes, how to find edible roots and berries and how to build weirs, or traps, to catch fish.

The courtyard of the Port Royal Habitation. Destroyed in 1613, the fort was rebuilt in the late 1930s according to Champlain's drawing.

By now the area had come to be called Acadia. The name may have come from "Arcadia," meaning a place of rural peace and simplicity; more likely it came from a Micmac word, "quoddy" or "cady" which meant a pleasant piece of land.

In 1607, de Monts' rights in Acadia were cancelled, and Port Royal was abandoned. In 1610, Jean de Biencourt de Poutrincourt, one of de Monts' companions, re-established the colony. Three years later, Samuel Argall, an adventurer from the English colony of Jamestown in Virginia, attacked and burned the small settlement. Thus England and France began their long struggle over Acadia.

In 1621, Sir William Alexander, a Scot, received a charter from the English king to settle Acadia. He renamed it "Nova Scotia" — New Scotland — and gave the colony its flag and coat of arms. Raising money by selling titles to anyone willing to pay, Alexander sent settlers to Port Royal and Cape Breton. However, in 1632 all the land he claimed was given back to France.

The Acadians

To the settlers it made little difference who claimed ownership of the land since both countries tended to neglect them between wars. Life in that new land created a new people — the Acadians. By 1650, about 300 French men and women had settled in and around the Annapolis Basin. Gradually they spread along the Bay of Fundy, Cobequid Bay and Minas Basin, and around the Chignecto Isthmus. By 1687, they numbered 2000. Working together, the Acadians built dykes along the tidal lands of the Bay of Fundy and turned the salt marshes behind them into fertile land. They grew hay, grain and vegetables and lived a self-sufficient life. They had large families, but did not cluster their houses together in European-style villages. Each Acadian family felt master of its own small plot of land.

The average house in Acadia was small by modern standards, with just one room and a loft overhead. The roof was made of thatch or sawn boards, and the small windows were usually covered with scraped animal skins or oiled paper.

Several times war broke out between the French and the English, and the colony changed hands. Through it all, the Acadians desperately tried to remain neutral — to avoid taking sides. Then in 1713, all of Acadia, except for Cape Breton Island, became British once and for all.

To guard the entrance to their empire on the St. Lawrence, the French built a mighty fortress at Louisbourg on Cape Breton Island. The fortress looked impressive, but it fell quickly in 1745 when it was attacked by New Englanders.

Meanwhile, Britain decided to establish a military base at Halifax. In 1749, Colonel Edward Cornwallis brought 2500 soldiers and

Building a dyke was a major undertaking. All the men in the community worked on it and then shared the all-important job of keeping it in good repair.

The original fortress of Louisbourg was destroyed by the British in 1760. Reconstruction began in 1961 and is still going on.

Costumed staff recreate daily life at the fort in the mid-1700s.

settlers to the harbour of Chebucto, laid out a townsite, and built a citadel on the hill overlooking the harbour. To further strengthen their control of Nova Scotia, the British decided to encourage new settlers. In 1753, 2500 "foreign Protestants" — mostly German and Swiss — arrived in Lunenburg.

By this time, there were 13 000 Acadians. British officials worried that they might side with the French if war broke out again. As tensions rose in Europe in the early 1750s, the governor, Charles Lawrence, demanded that the Acadians sign an oath of loyalty to the British Crown. They refused. And so began a shameful episode in Canadian history.

In 1755, Governor Lawrence ordered all Acadians deported. Soldiers swept down on the peaceful farms. Acadian families

The same scene before and after the expulsion of the Acadians. British soldiers burned churches, farm buildings and crops so that there would be nothing for anyone who escaped deportation to come back to.

watched as their houses and the crops in their carefully tended fields went up in flames. Some escaped into the woods. Ships arrived at Grand Pré to take the others into exile. Families were torn apart as 10 000 Acadians were scattered among Britain's other North American colonies. The journey for many was terrible. One ship left Chignecto carrying 417 people. By the time it reached South Carolina, half of them had died of disease and despair.

When war broke out in 1756, Governor Lawrence encouraged settlers from New England to come and take over Acadian lands.

Between 1760 and 1763, when the war ended, about 4500 "New England Planters" arrived in Nova Scotia.

New Arrivals

During the war, the British took Louisbourg — which had reverted to France during the brief peace — in 1758. A year later they attacked Quebec City and captured the whole of New France. Under the Treaty of Paris, which ended the war, Britain added Ile Royale (Cape Breton Island) and Ile St-Jean (Prince Edward Island) to Nova Scotia. Prince Edward Island, however, became a separate colony in 1769.

Acadians began to return even before the war ended. By 1801, they numbered 8000 — about half of them in Nova Scotia. Many settled on land given to them in the southwestern part of the province, in an area now known as the "French Shore." Here they re-established their homes, fished, farmed and cut wood. But the Acadians were now a minority in Nova Scotia.

In 1772-73, 1000 settlers from Yorkshire, England, arrived at Chignecto, and 200 Scots landed at Pictou in 1773. After the American War of Independence (1775-1783), about 35 000 people who remained loyal to the British Crown, including 3000 Blacks, came to Nova Scotia.

Some 14 000 Loyalists settled in the Saint John River valley. They soon became unhappy with having their affairs run from Halifax and put pressure on the British government to split Nova Scotia into two colonies. In 1784 Britain agreed, and New Brunswick became a separate colony. At the same time, Cape Breton was also split off, but it was rejoined to Nova Scotia in 1820.

The 20 000 Loyalists who landed in southwest Nova Scotia had visions of creating a new Boston in Shelburne. But the hostile soil could not sustain the needs of the newcomers. Some returned to the United States, others moved to England, muttering about "Nova Scarcity." But many stayed.

Left: A shipload of Loyalists arrive in Nova Scotia. *Below*: A view of Halifax Harbour in the 1770s. A census taken about that time classified the residents of the Halifax area as follows: 1352 Americans, 855 Irish, 302 English, 264 Germans and other Protestants, 200 Acadians, 52 Scots and 44 Blacks.

The *Hector* lands in 1773 with the first group of Scottish families to settle in the Pictou area. A full-size replica of the *Hector* is currently being built at Pictou as part of a Pictou Harbour development plan.

The black Loyalists founded their own community at Birchtown and gradually spread throughout the province. Their life was very hard, and in 1792 some accepted an offer of free passage to Africa. Most, however, stayed and struggled to make a living in this difficult land.

Between 1815 and 1825, the first small group of Scottish settlers at Pictou were joined by at least 9000 Highland Scots. These Gaelic-speaking Scots were tenant farmers who had been forced from their homes by landlords who wanted the land for sheep.

Scottish Cape Bretoners are very proud of their heritage. Many towns and villages celebrate with Highland Days featuring traditional games, music and dancing.

More than 2000 of the Scottish Highlanders settled in Cape Breton where there was land for the taking — and no landlords. The first comers settled the most fertile lands along the river valleys. As more than 7000 new Scottish settlers arrived on the island over the next few years, many had to settle on the "backlands," where the soil was poor. Undaunted, the Scots set about recreating their Gaelic communities and making a better life for themselves and their children. These days, parts of Cape Breton are more Scottish than Scotland!

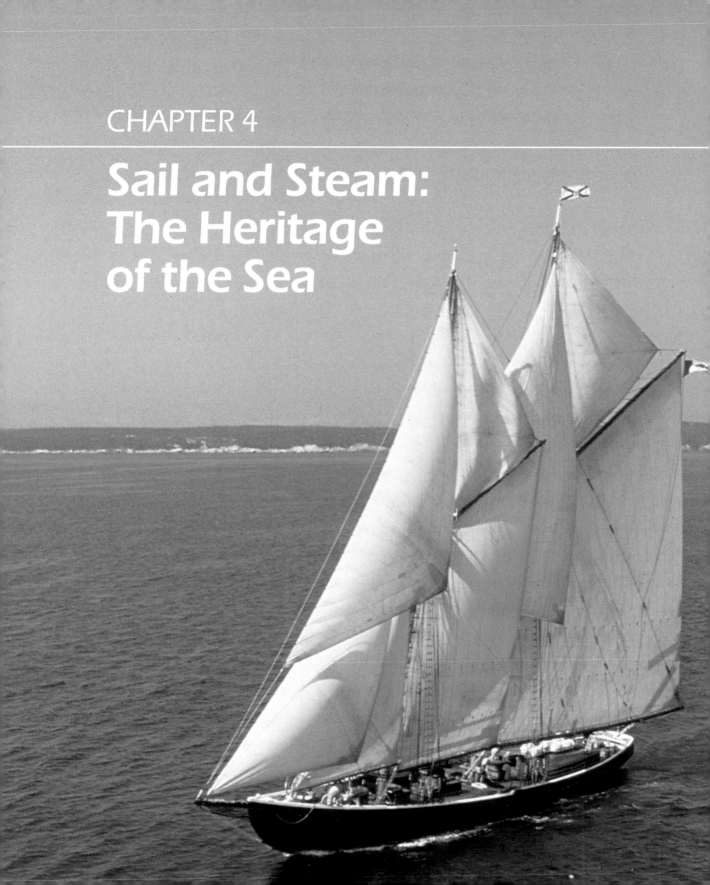

CHAPTER 4

Sail and Steam: The Heritage of the Sea

Many of the newcomers turned their hand to farming. The Annapolis Valley, the Chignecto Isthmus and the shores of Northumberland Strait rewarded hard work with good crops. Elsewhere the rocky, acid soil yielded poor harvests.

Increasingly Nova Scotians turned to the sea for food and a living. They cut the tall white pine to build ships and ventured farther and farther from the colony's shores to fish and trade. During the eighteenth century Nova Scotia ships carried fish to the West Indies and returned with sugar, molasses and rum. And when Britain went to war during the second half of the century, Nova Scotian merchants and captains found another way of making money — privateering.

Privateers obtained *letters of marque* from the governor that allowed them to attack and capture enemy ships. Between 1756 and 1815 converted merchant ships sailed from Halifax, Shelburne, Liverpool and Annapolis Royal to attack French, American and other vessels belonging to the King's enemies. Profits from the sale of the captured ships and their contents laid the foundations of several Nova Scotia fortunes. Enos Collins, born in Liverpool in 1774, captained a trading vessel at nineteen. During the War of 1812 with the United States, he sent out privateers to capture American ships. He was so successful that he moved to Halifax and started his own bank (the building still stands on the waterfront). He died in 1871 — one of the richest men in Canada.

The schooner *Bluenose* lost only one race in her remarkable career. The ship's likeness can be seen on the back of the Canadian dime. *Bluenose II*, shown here, is a replica built in 1963.

The number of ships wrecked around Sable Island have earned it the nickname "The Graveyard of the Atlantic." *Inset*: The *Crofton Hall*, wrecked on Sable Island, with its ironclad hull broken amidships.

During the nineteenth century shipyards were established in many coves and inlets. The Churchill shipyard at Hantsport was once the fifth largest in the world. Sea captains built fine houses and filled them with oriental screens, teakwood chests, china tea sets and other articles brought from the far corners of the world.

Life at sea offered rewards. But it also took its toll. Over four thousand wrecks lie around the coasts of the province. Sable Island became known as "The Graveyard of the Atlantic." A memorial in Lunenburg lists the names of a hundred ships lost at sea from that port alone. Many old houses in Nova Scotia have "widow's walks" on their roofs. Here the wives of captains gazed out to sea, searching the horizon for the sails of their husbands' ships. Captains often took their wives and children on voyages, and the sea claimed their lives too.

Ship's captains drove their men hard and many sailors died in accidents and from disease. Even so, young men could not wait to join a ship. Benjamin Doane of Barrington, born in 1823, worked on

the family farm as a boy but his heart was not in it. Just before his
fifteenth birthday, he shipped out as a cook on a small schooner. At
nineteen he went to sea with a whaler. For three and a half months
of hard living and hard work he earned $20.40 and half a barrel of
oil. Still, four years later Doane signed on for a two-and-a-half-year
whaling voyage, eagerly wondering "what strange lands [the ship]
would bear me to; what dangers I should meet."

Yarmouth's Pride

Until about 1881, Nova Scotia had the largest tonnage of shipping,
per person, in the world. For a time in the middle of the nineteenth
century, Yarmouth was the second largest shipping port in Canada
and one of the largest in the British Empire. Thirty local shipyards
built sturdy vessels. Local merchants established banks and insurance companies to finance their ventures and protect them against
the loss of ships and cargoes. Risk was also shared by selling shares
in ships.

Boys and girls watched vessels arriving in Yarmouth to be rigged and fitted for sea. Girls, it was said, could talk ship and name sails as well as boys. Vessels ranged from schooners of 20 tonnes (22 tons) to ships eighty times that size. Their captains became local heroes and role models. Every boy wanted to be a sailor — and hoped to end his days at sea as captain of a large vessel.

To some extent, the very success of sailing ships throughout the middle years of the nineteenth century would be their downfall. Steamships made of iron would soon take over the industry, but most Nova Scotian shipowners had all their money tied up in wooden ships. As long as they were still doing well they were reluctant to take new risks.

The Arrival of Steam

One Nova Scotian saw the shape of the future and made his fortune with iron ships. Samuel Cunard, born in Halifax in 1797, was described as a man "who made both men and things bend to his will." Cunard joined his father's timber business and helped expand it into whaling, coal and iron, and shipping. In 1839 he founded the British and North American Royal Mail Packet Company to carry mail by steamship from England to Halifax, Quebec City and Boston. On July 4, 1840, the company's paddlewheeler *Britannia* left Liverpool, beginning regular mail service across the Atlantic by steamer. The ship took twelve days to reach Halifax. In 1855 the company began using iron ships and in the 1860s Cunard replaced paddle wheelers with vessels driven by screw propellers.

In the second half of the nineteenth century shipping companies competed with each other to make the speediest crossing of the Atlantic. On April 1, 1873, the two-year old White Star liner *Atlantic*, carrying 933 passengers and crew, hit Meagher's Rock just outside Halifax Harbour. She had burned too much coal in her race to New York and headed for Halifax to refuel. Despite heroic rescue efforts by the fishermen of Prospect, 562 of those on board drowned in the angry sea. Except for one boy of twelve, all the women and children died.

The End of an Era: Great Ships

As steam replaced sail, shipyards around the province closed, wharves rotted, and an industry died. Halifax and Sydney became coaling ports. Ports such as Digby, Canso and Lunenburg kept their importance as fishing centres.

The tradition of building wooden ships continued for a time even as white sails gave way to black funnels. Many people assured William Lawrence of Maitland that he was making a mistake when he began building the very large sailing ship that carried his name. The *William D. Lawrence* slid into the water in 1874 amid great re-

The *William D. Lawrence*, launched in October 1874, was the largest wooden sailing ship ever built in the Maritimes.

joicing for ship launchings were festive events in every community. Lawrence took her on a voyage around the world and made a healthy profit for the eight years he kept her. The "Great Ship" ended her days as a barge in West Africa.

In 1921 the Rhuland shipyard in Lunenburg launched the 47-metre (154-foot) "salt banker" *Bluenose*. The schooner had beautiful lines and moved gracefully through the water. *Bluenose* brought back record hauls of fish from the Grand Banks of Newfoundland. In competitions with schooners from Nova Scotia and New England, *Bluenose* won the International Fisherman's Trophy in 1921, 1922, 1923, 1931 and 1938. She lost a race only once. The vessel hit a reef and sank off Haiti while carrying cargo in 1946. The Canadian dime carries an engraving of this most famous of schooners.

New Opportunities

One of the most colourful periods in Nova Scotia's sea history came during the 1920s when the American government banned the manufacture and sale of beer, wine and spirits. Prohibition, as it was called, offered new opportunities for some Nova Scotia seamen. Using their sailing skills and knowledge of the coastline, they smuggled cargoes of whiskey, rum, brandy and other beverages in schooners and fast motorboats to American buyers. American Coast Guard cutters and the Royal Canadian Mounted Police (RCMP) Marine Division tried to stop the smuggling, but with little success.

Although illegal, rum-running was attractive to many Nova Scotians. Hugh Corkum went to sea at the age of fifteen. Out of work, he was offered $75 a month by the RCMP to serve as a radio operator. Instead, he shipped aboard a rum-runner for $300 a month. When he married, his wife urged him to quit the illegal trade and in 1939 he joined the Lunenburg police force for $65 a month. He eventually became the town's police chief — and its truant officer, tax collector, sanitary inspector, provincial constable, fence viewer and deputy fire marshal!

Left: The corvette HMCS *Battleford* on convoy duty. *Above*: HMCS *Lunenburg*. During winter storms, water sweeping over a corvette's deck froze, and crew-members had to hack the ice off to keep the ship from becoming topheavy and rolling over.

The port of Halifax boomed during both the First and Second World wars. Between 1914 and 1918 troopships took soldiers to the battlefields in Europe and hospital ships returned with men shattered in body and mind. During the Second World War convoys assembled in Bedford Basin as German submarines waited outside the harbour entrance to prey on allied ships. Halifax once again became a centre for shipbuilding and repair.

After the Second World War passenger liners continued to call at Halifax. Many immigrants landed here on their way to a new life in a new country. But gradually more and more people crossed the Atlantic by air, and passenger liners all but vanished from the oceans of the world. Summer cruise ships are now the only passenger ships that call at Halifax.

In 1959, the opening of the St. Lawrence Seaway diverted much shipping traffic from Halifax to Montreal and Great Lakes ports. As well, east coast American ports began to modernize. Halifax was in danger of losing its role as a world port. To save it, business people

Above: The Halifax naval base. *Left*:
Container ships at Halifax Harbour. The
port of Halifax handles over 250 000
containers a year.

turned to a new technology — containers. Containerization means
a lot less handling because the goods for one destination are packed
at the source and delivered without being unpacked.

In 1970 the first container pier opened at the entrance to the harbour and a second one at Bedford Basin began operations in 1982.
About thirty container lines use the piers. A quarter of the 13 mil-

The distinctive red-and-white vessels of the Canadian Coast Guard
at Dartmouth. Members of the Coast Guard are trained at the
Canadian Coast Guard College at Sydney.

lion metric tons of freight handled at Halifax in 1995 came in containers.

At one time Halifax Harbour resembled a forest, with the masts
of ships crowding the wharves. Now, naval vessels slide in and out
of the harbour, giant cranes load and unload containers, tankers
take on and discharge oil at the Dartmouth refinery, and huge ships
deliver hundreds of cars to the autoport at Eastern Passage. And
yet the vast expanse of water seems strangely empty.

Bluenose II, a replica of the original vessel, takes visitors around
the harbour in summer. And along the South Shore a few dedicated
people still make wooden boats, keeping alive a vital part of the
province's heritage and the memory of the days of sail.

CHAPTER 5

Social and Economic Development to 1945

As its maritime history shows, Nova Scotia always had plenty of enterprising people. But their efforts were often hampered by government policy, small markets at home and the interests of powerful people.

Most Nova Scotians lived self-contained lives in scattered settlements. When Thomas McCulloch, the Scottish preacher and educator, arrived in Pictou in 1803 it consisted of a private wharf, several taverns, one or two stores, a shipyard, a jail and a smithy — but no church. By 1816, he was able to write, "The country is settling and improving with amazing rapidity."

Travel was slow in those early days, and sometimes difficult. The Great North Road linked Halifax with Windsor, and the Old Cobequid Road connected it with Truro and Pictou. Travellers in more remote parts of the province went on foot or in canoes during the summer and on snowshoes in winter. In the 1830s the Great Road was extended down the Annapolis Valley, but it took sixteen hours, with an overnight stop, for the stagecoach to go from Halifax to Annapolis Royal.

For a long time, the British government restricted the development of the colony by insisting that it produce nothing that competed with the home country. North America's first coal mine opened at Port Morien on Cape Breton in 1720 while France still controlled the island. Later, the British government allowed coal to be mined only for local needs — not for export.

In 1825 the General Mining Association was formed. Two years later it took over the mines in the Sydney area and stepped up

In his 1925 painting called *Miners' Houses, Glace Bay*, artist Lawren Harris captured the bleak and barren world of Cape Breton mining towns.

production. In 1839 the Association built the first railway line in Atlantic Canada near Pictou. On cast iron rails Nova Scotia's first locomotive, the *Samson*, hauled coal to waiting ships.

In 1832 the Bank of Nova Scotia, Canada's second-oldest chartered bank, opened in Halifax. Between 1826 and 1840 the province's population doubled. A sense of optimism began to grow as the shipping industry prospered.

The Railway Era

Railways were seen as the key to provincial development. Joseph Howe, Nova Scotia's dominant political figure of the mid-nineteenth century, tried unsuccessfully to convince the British government to guarantee a loan for a railway from Halifax to Portland in Maine and then on to Quebec City. In 1854 a railway did link Halifax with Windsor and Truro, but four years later the province still had only 240 kilometres (150 miles) of track. The railway era in Nova Scotia really began after 1867. One of the conditions for Nova Scotia's joining Confederation was the building of the Intercolonial Railway. This would close the gap between Rivière-du-Loup in Quebec and Truro. The line between the two communities opened for traffic in July 1876. At the same time the Dominion government took over all the railways built by the Nova Scotia government.

The *Samson*, Canada's oldest steam engine, hauled coal from the mines around Pictou to the harbour. It is now on display in the Museum of Industry at Stellarton.

The middle years of the nineteenth century were good for Nova Scotia. Population continued to grow. The standard of living rose. Improved transportation created markets for new goods and speeded them on their way.

New Industries

One of the success stories was the founding of Oland's Breweries. John and Susannah Oland had a comfortable life in England where John Oland worked for a railway. Officials invited him to organize and run the Nova Scotia Railway. The Oland family settled in Dartmouth in 1862. Susannah Oland began to serve guests a special ale that she brewed. A friend suggested it be put on the market, and on October 1, 1867, the Olands opened the Army and Navy Brewery. When John died in a riding accident, Susannah took over the company and ran it successfully.

Other manufacturing companies opened. In 1866, the Starr Manufacturing Company in Dartmouth began making skates that became world-famous. Two years later, the Stanfield textile mill in Truro opened, and Canada's first steelmaking plant opened in New Glasgow in 1883. Amherst became an important industrial centre with a railway-car works, an engineering company and factories making woolen goods, enamel products, footwear and pianos.

New coal mines opened in Springhill in 1872. Although living and working conditions in the coal mining communities on the mainland and in Cape Breton were terrible, they attracted people in search of regular employment.

Henry Melville Whitney, a Boston financier, took over the coal mines around Sydney in 1893. Five years later he founded the Dominion Iron and Steel company to use some of the coal, and its mill began operations in 1901. Another steel plant was established at Sydney Mines in the first years of the twentieth century. Men left farms and small communities to work in the mines and the mills, and between 1900 and 1910 the province prospered.

In rural areas, life went on much as it always had. Every community had skilled craftspeople who produced by hand the things used in everyday life. In 1880-81 a hundred coopers made barrels in Nova Scotia and the province had over a thousand blacksmiths. With the coming of machines these jobs disappeared. But some craft-based ventures survived. The Dominion Chair Company in Bass River started around 1870 and sold its products all across Canada and abroad. It remains in business to this day.

The First World War

When war between Britain and Germany broke out in August 1914, it brought boom times to Halifax but stripped the province of some of its finest young men. The enlistment rate for Nova Scotia was one of the highest in Canada. Black Nova Scotians were enlisted in a special Construction Battalion that did valuable support work for the front-line troops.

Defence activities helped the local economy. Halifax became a base for shipping supplies and troops to Europe. Of the 425 000

The Halifax Explosion shattered windows 80 km (50 mi.) away and created a shock wave that was felt all the way to Sydney, on Cape Breton Island.

Canadians who went overseas between 1914 and 1918, 3 of every 4 passed through the port. The small Canadian navy patrolled the coasts of the province and American submarine chasers docked in Halifax. Industries in Halifax and Dartmouth produced sugar, textiles, iron and steel and other goods.

Then, on the morning of December 6, 1917, the war came to Halifax. Two ships collided in the Narrows between the harbour and Bedford Basin. People gathered on wharves, and at house windows to watch as one ship drifted towards shore and a plume of smoke arose from the other. The drifting ship, the *Imo*, was a Belgian relief steamer. The other, the French vessel *Mont Blanc*, carried explosives. Sparks from the collision set fire to benzol on the *Mont Blanc's* deck, and at 9:06 a.m. the ship exploded. The blast levelled the North End of Halifax, killing 2000 people and injuring 9000 others. Many hundreds standing at windows were blinded by flying glass. The sugar refinery on the waterfront collapsed, the Dominion Textile plant became rubble, and ships in the harbour were tossed around like toys in a baby's bath. Stoves in wooden houses started fires that burned until midnight.

The Halifax Explosion was the largest man-made explosion until 1945 when the atomic bomb was dropped on Hiroshima. Search and rescue parties began to work among the wreckage within half an hour and continued for days. King George V sent his sympathy. Australia, New Zealand, London, New York and Chicago sent money. Relief trains from New York City and Boston rushed supplies, food, doctors and nurses to the stricken city.

The Postwar Years

The end of the war brought hard times to Nova Scotia. A depression that began in 1921 sent many Nova Scotians looking for work in other parts of Canada and in the United States. The federal government cut back on military expenditure. Farmers lost their markets. The steel plant in Sydney Mines closed in 1920 and condi-

This cartoon expresses the bitterness Cape Breton coal miners felt about their treatment at the hands of BESCO — the British Empire Steel Corporation — which owned all the coal mines and steel mills in Nova Scotia.

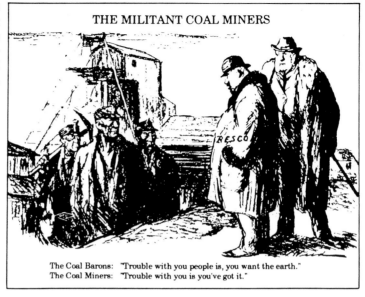

THE MILITANT COAL MINERS

The Coal Barons: "Trouble with you people is, you want the earth."
The Coal Miners: "Trouble with you is you've got it."

tions in the coalfields became wretched. Miners and their families lived in company-owned houses and had to buy what they needed from company-owned stores, known as "pluck-me's." One man at Glace Bay was paid $34.43 for a month's work. By the time he had paid his rent, his store account, and deductions for supplies and fees, his take-home pay came to 70 cents.

During the 1920s the mining companies decided to cut the workers' pay. Discontent rose among the miners, and led by the fiery James B. McLachlan, they went on strike in 1922, 1923 and 1925. The federal government sent soldiers to protect the mines and stores from the strikers, who were desperate because their families were starving. On June 11, 1925, company police fired on a demonstration at New Waterford. William Davis, a coal miner, fell dead. He is remembered in Cape Breton on Miners' Memorial Day, on the anniversary of his death.

During the thirties the economy of Nova Scotia continued to suffer. Factories in Amherst and elsewhere closed as markets shrank.

The provincial government created work by paving 1600 kilometres (1000 miles) of roads between 1933 and 1940. It also promoted tourism. The federal government created Cape Breton Highlands National Park in 1939 to attract visitors, generate jobs and protect the environment.

In rural areas people came together to solve their problems through co-operation. In 1928 Father Moses Michael Coady of St. Francis Xavier University in Antigonish preached the gospel of self-help in eastern Nova Scotia. Fishermen and farmers pooled their nickels and dimes, formed study clubs and started credit unions and co-operatives. They sold their fish, lobster and lambs for better prices and paid less for their supplies. In 1939 Coady published *Masters of Their Own Destiny*, the story of what became known world-wide as the Antigonish Movement.

The Second World War

By the time Coady's book appeared, the world again stood on the edge of war. The Second World War brought another boom to Nova Scotia. Windsor and Debert grew as large troop camps were built nearby. Halifax, known for security purposes as "an East Coast Port," became the centre for naval operations in the Western Atlantic. Convoys assembled in Bedford Basin and set off for Britain across seas in which German submarines lurked. Halifax and Pictou shipyards built destroyers using Nova Scotia steel. At the steel plant in Sydney, women replaced men in the rail mill.

Three Nova Scotia battalions — the North Novas, West Novas and Cape Breton Highlanders — fought bravely in the Italian campaign and in northwestern Europe.

When the European war officially ended on May 7, 1945, the tensions in the overcrowded city of Halifax exploded and celebration turned into riots. Stores were looted and 200 people were arrested. When it was over, the city and the province settled down to face the challenges of peace.

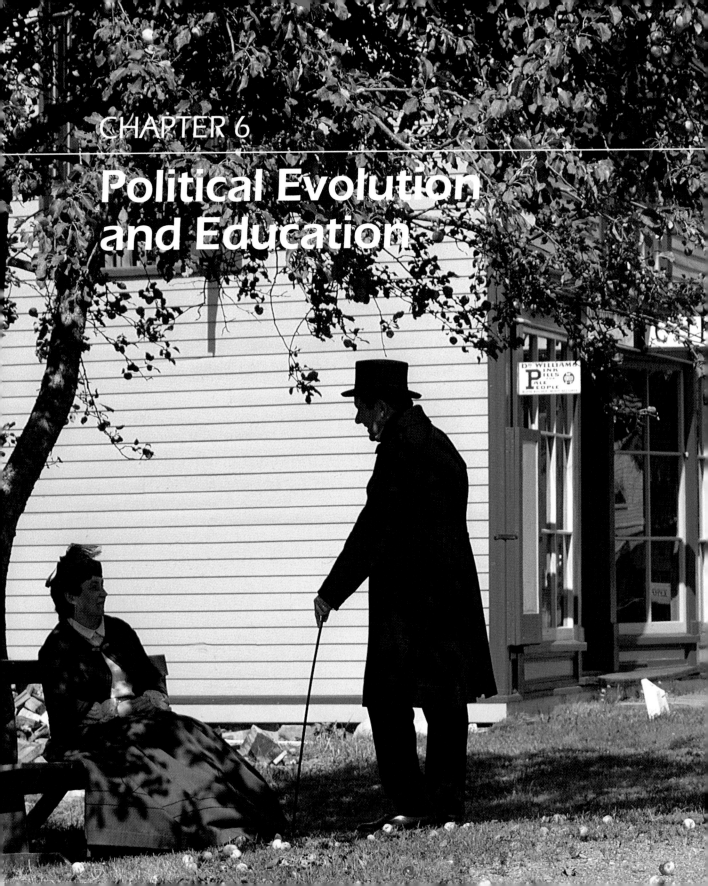

CHAPTER 6

Political Evolution and Education

The colony of Nova Scotia had the first elected assembly in the British Empire. Set up in 1758, its members were elected by male Protestant landowners over twenty-one years of age. However, the governor and his appointed council of advisors were not accountable to this assembly. They ran the colony to meet their own needs.

When the Loyalists arrived they objected to this system. Their leaders had been men of wealth and privilege before coming to Nova Scotia. They demanded a voice in governing the colony. Then in 1792 John Wentworth, a Loyalist, became governor. He appointed his Loyalist friends to the council. They were now the ones who gave out land grants and government benefits to friends, and made sure that their own interests were protected.

In theory, the governor and his council were supposed to consult the elected assembly when they wanted to spend money. In practice, they ignored it. Demands for reform increased after the War of 1812 ended. The new middle class made up of professionals such as lawyers, doctors and small business people wanted the governor and his council to be responsible to all Nova Scotians, not just to small groups of wealthy and powerful men.

Joseph Howe

One of the most important Nova Scotians of this time was Joseph Howe. He was born in 1804 in a modest cottage in Halifax. When he died in 1873, he was lieutenant-governor of his beloved Nova

Life in the 1860s as re-enacted at Sherbrooke Village

After successfully defending himself against charges of libel, Joseph Howe is carried out of the courthouse on the shoulders of his admirers.

Scotia. Howe dominated political life through much of the nineteenth century. He was an able politician, a splendid speaker, a courageous newspaper editor, and one of Nova Scotia's genuine folk heroes.

Howe used his newspaper, the *Novascotian*, to call for reform. On January 1, 1835, he ran a letter in the paper calling the members of the governor's council little better than thieves. Sued for libel, Howe defended himself in a famous trial and was acquitted. His victory secured the freedom of the press — newspapers could now criticize government without fear.

Elected to the assembly in 1836, Howe demanded that the laws governing Nova Scotians be made by this body and not by the governor and his friends. The governor should select his advisers from "those who enjoy the confidence of the people and can command a majority in the popular branch."

In 1848 the battle was won. The governor was told by the British government to choose his council, or ministers, from the group that had a majority in the assembly. James B. Uniacke became first minister, or premier. Joseph Howe was made provincial secretary in the first *responsible government* in a British colony. This had been achieved, in Howe's words, without "a blow struck or a pane of glass broken."

But Howe lost his next battle. Originally, he had favoured a union of the British North American colonies. However, he opposed Confederation when it came in the 1860s because the voters in Nova Scotia had not been consulted. Nova Scotians elected nineteen members to Canada's first House of Commons in 1867. Eighteen of them were determined to pull Nova Scotia out of Confederation. Howe was one of them, but there was little he could do. He finally abandoned his opposition when Sir John A. Macdonald, the new Dominion's first prime minister offered him a cabinet post and a better deal for Nova Scotia.

Three Nova Scotian Prime Ministers

The man who brought Nova Scotia into Confederation was Charles Tupper. Tupper became premier in 1864, and was the champion of British North American union. In 1867 he went to Parliament as the sole supporter of Confederation from Nova Scotia. He played a prominent role in federal politics, and was prime minister briefly in 1896.

Four years earlier another Nova Scotian had held the post of prime minister. John Thompson served briefly as premier of Nova Scotia and then joined Sir John A. Macdonald's government as minister of justice in 1885. In 1892 he became prime minister of Canada. Morally courageous and forceful, Thompson died two years later at Windsor Castle, an hour after being sworn in as member of the Imperial Privy Council by Queen Victoria.

Sir John Thompson, prime minister of Canada, 1892-4. Thompson died after just two years in office. He is best remembered for drawing up Canada's Criminal Code while serving as minister of justice in Sir John A. Macdonald's cabinet.

Sir Robert Borden, prime minister of Canada 1911-20. Borden took Canada an important step forward on the way to independence by insisting that the country's major contribution to the war effort had earned it a voice of its own in world affairs.

Robert Borden, the third prime minister from Nova Scotia, served from 1911 to 1920, a crucial period in Canadian history. Like Tupper and Thompson, he was a Conservative. Borden supported a strong role for Canadian troops during the First World War. After the war, he played a leading part in the creation of the British Commonwealth of Nations as a partnership of equals.

Tupper, Thompson and Borden were all knighted. With typical Nova Scotian modesty, Borden told his nephew a few hours before his death in 1937: "Remember, Henry, none of this "sir" stuff at the cemetery." His tombstone carries only his name and the dates of his birth and death.

Governing Nova Scotia

Once Nova Scotians acquired responsible government, the fire seemed to go out of politics. A university professor born in the

A statue of Joseph Howe stands outside Province House, where Nova Scotia's first
responsible government met on February 2, 1848. Opened in 1819, Province House
is the oldest legislative building in the country.

province noted: "Nova Scotians have a tendency in politics to seek
leaders and then, having found them, to follow each with a loyalty
often not understood by outsiders."

Nova Scotian governments tend to be long-lasting. Up to 1956,
the province had a Liberal government for sixty-six of seventy-four
years. In 1920, a radical party of farmers and labour supporters won
eleven seats in the politically conservative province. But most Nova
Scotians continued to vote Liberals or Conservatives into office.

Some premiers have been outstanding men. Angus L. Macdonald
became Liberal premier in 1933 and worked hard to limit the mis-
ery that the Great Depression brought to the province. He went to
Ottawa as minister of the navy when war broke out in 1939, then returned to lead the province as it recovered from the war. Much
loved by Nova Scotians, he died in 1954, worn out by hard work.

Two years later, Robert Stanfield led the Conservatives to victory
at the polls. For the next eleven years, he worked hard to make

Nova Scotia more self-reliant. He left provincial politics in 1967 to become leader of the federal Progressive Conservative Party. After failing three times in his bid to become Canada's fourth Nova Scotian prime minister, Stanfield retired from politics in 1976. A highly intelligent man with a quiet wit, he has been described as "the best prime minister Canada never had."

In 1970 the provincial Liberals took power in Nova Scotia under Gerald Regan. His government brought in important labour, environmental and health legislation. In 1978, the Conservatives under John Buchanan won the election. His government continued to support oil and gas projects and a tidal power project on the Annapolis River. Dozens of school boards were amalgamated and Acadians were given the right to French-lanaguage education. Buchanan served as premier until 1990 when he was appointed to the Canadian Senate. In 1993, a Liberal government under Dr. John Savage took office after winning 41 of the 52 seats in the legislature.

Education

Nova Scotians have a high regard for learning. The province has more universities for its size than any other province.

Charles Tupper took the lead in bringing free schools to the province. In 1864 and 1865 acts requiring the opening of schools without payment of fees were passed. Local people had to pay taxes to build the schools and pay the teachers.

One-room schools emerged in every community. Teachers received $125 a term. They moved from house to house as guests of the owners, paying no board. Boys often left school after Grade 3 to help on the farms. Girls stayed in school longer.

Early educators made great efforts to create a college system that would be open to all. King's College, founded in Windsor in 1789, took only Anglican students. Two years after Thomas McCulloch arrived in Pictou in 1803 he formed a society to bring into being "a college of learning" open to everyone. Pictou Academy became a

Acadia University, Wolfville. Founded by Baptists, Acadia is now a non-denominational college with about 4000 students. *Inset*: Sir Charles Tupper. In addition to providing Nova Scotians with free public school education, Tupper took the province into Confederation, held several positions in the federal cabinet and served briefly as prime minister in 1896.

reality in 1816. A year later Dalhousie University opened its doors in Halifax. Like Pictou Academy, it took students from all religions. Dalhousie has grown into the largest university in Atlantic Canada. Pictou Academy, however, never achieved university status.

The dream of universities without religious ties faded as denominations started their own colleges throughout the province. In 1828, Baptists established Horton Academy in Wolfville and then, ten years later, Queen's College, which became Acadia University. Catholics in Halifax founded Saint Mary's University, and those in eastern Nova Scotia started St. Francis Xavier College. The Sisters of Charity opened a women's academy, now Mount Saint Vincent University, on the shores of Bedford Basin in 1873. Université Ste-Anne at Church Point on the French Shore opened in 1890.

These colleges offered a liberal education, but Dalhousie also trained doctors and lawyers. The need for specialized eduction for agriculture and industry led to the creation of the Nova Scotia Agricultural College in Truro in 1905 and the Nova Scotia Technical College (now a university) in Halifax two years later. The Nova Scotia College of Art and Design was founded in 1887.

In recent years there has been increased co-operation between the universities in Nova Scotia. In 1971 Catholics, Anglicans and United Church members came together to establish the Atlantic School of Theology, the first such theological college in Canada.

Recently, the province has established a system of community colleges for students who do not wish to pursue university education.

Local Government

There was little "local" government in Nova Scotia until Halifax became a city in 1841. Dartmouth followed suit in 1873. The residents of Pictou, Truro, New Glasgow and Windsor took control of their own affairs over the next five years.

In 1879 the province created eighteen counties. Local government changed little since these counties were created until the mid-nineties. Then the new Liberal government began to reform the system. By April 1, 1996, 66 municipal units had been reduced to 55.

Regional municipalities cover Industrial Cape Breton, the Halifax-Dartmouth-Bedford area, and the town of Liverpool and Queens County. This move reduced the number of elected officials in these parts of the province by two thirds. In rural municipalities mem-

The city of Sydney Civic Centre, a four-storey, multi-function building constructed in 1976. The Police Station is located on the first floor, while City Council holds its meetings in the round council chamber seen here.

bers represent districts and elect one of their number as warden to preside over council meetings. Mayors in cities are directly elected.

Until recently, Nova Scotia had an unusual system for selecting school boards — only one-third of the members were elected by registered voters, the rest were appointed. In 1991, the province changed to a system of fully elected school boards.

CHAPTER 7
The Modern Economy

Nova Scotia prospered during the Second World War, but it did not share in the postwar boom. More and more Nova Scotians moved to Ontario and the Canadian West looking for work. Between 1956 and 1966, 60 000 Nova Scotians "went down the road." In an effort to stop the drain of young people, the Stanfield government established Industrial Estates Ltd. to bring new businesses to Nova Scotia. Michelin Tire established three tire manufacturing plants at Waterville, Granton and Bridgewater during the 1960s and 1970s. But other ventures proved less successful.

Cape Breton was especially hard hit by high unemployment. As oil replaced coal as Canada's main fuel, coal mines shut down. To help preserve the jobs of the miners, the federal government set up the Cape Breton Development Corporation (DEVCO) in 1967 to operate the coal mines and to start new industries. On "Black Friday," October 13, 1967, Cape Breton's other major employer, the steel plant, announced that it was closing. Again to save jobs, the provincial government bought the mill. At the time, it employed 3500 workers. Now only a few hundred workers operate the mill, which has become a joint venture with a Chinese company.

Employment in the service sector has increased throughout Nova Scotia. Only about a quarter of the labour force now produces goods. The rest work in government, trade, communications, transportation, the armed forces, schools and universities. The sons and daughters of fishermen and farmers operate computers, nurse the

The World Trade and Convention Centre, Halifax, is recognizable by its huge weathervane. This complex incorporates the 10 000-seat Metro Centre, which hosts concerts, sports and trade shows.

sick, sell insurance and police the streets of the province. Nova Scotia has three times as many teachers as coal miners.

The failures of businesses started by people from "away" has forced the provincial and federal governments to look for more effective ways of creating jobs. They now seek to encourage local enterprise, entrepreneurship and small business. Great changes have taken place in fishing, forestry and farming. Everyone involved has had to use new equipment and seek new markets to stay in business.

Fishing, Forestry and Farming

Fishing remains a major industry in Nova Scotia, with exports of almost $800 million in 1995. The industry boomed after 1977 when the Canadian government extended its territorial control to the 200-mile limit beyond its coastline. However, expansion of fishing fleets led to overfishing and the decline of fish stocks. As a result, many fish processing plants in communities like Canso, Lockeport and Digby were threatened. In 1993, the closure of the cod fisheries threw 6000 Nova Scotians out of work.

The industry employed 13 636 workers in 1995 on fishing vessels and in processing plants. Inshore fishermen go out each day to catch cod and other species, and to set and collect lobster pots. Large fishing trawlers bring fish to the plants, which provide work for many women in many small communities. Scallop draggers from Digby rake the seafloor to harvest shellfish. The lobster, which at one time was considered poor people's food, is now a major part of the fishery. Jets leave Halifax International Airport with lobsters to supply restaurants in Europe and the United States.

About half of the fishing catch consisted of cod, haddock, pollock and redfish in 1995. Much of this was exported in frozen blocks to the United States. Increasingly the fish companies are seeking to turn raw fish into new products, and the government is encourag-

Left: A lone fishing boat heads out to sea in the Bay of Fundy. *Above*: Picking strawberries in Oxford, Cumberland County, home of the annual mid-July Strawberry Festival

ing the catching of neglected species such as hake. Interest is rising in aquaculture, and fish farms in Nova Scotia now raise Atlantic salmon, trout, mussels and oysters.

The province exported $726 million worth of wood pulp and paper in 1995. Mills at Brooklyn, Liverpool, Port Hawkesbury and Abercrombie are supplied by the 2000 workers who cut wood in the forests. Like inshore fishing, work in the woods is seasonal. Dozens of small sawmills throughout the province turn out lumber for construction. Nova Scotia exports about nine million Christmas trees each year.

Agriculture has changed greatly since the war. As in many parts of Canada, farms have been abandoned. The current annual harvest of apples in the Annapolis Valley is only a third of what was produced in the 1930s. Then much of the crop was sold in Britain; today it is sold mainly in Atlantic Canada. Valley farmers also grow pears, strawberries and vegetables that are sold fresh, frozen and canned.

Dairy cows grazing near Grand Pré. *Inset*: Howard Dill, Guinness World Record holder, poses with one of his giant pumpkins during the World Pumpkin Festival held each Thanksgiving Day in Windsor.

Dairying accounts for just over a quarter of the total farm cash income of around $300 million a year. Poultry and hog farms serve local markets. The province has an ideal climate for hay, which is grown for local use and export.

Some farmers specialize. There are several mink farms in Digby County, and other farmers in the province grow tobacco. Grapes from the Valley's vineyards are made into wine, and Oxford, in Cumberland County, is known as "The Blueberry Capital of Canada."

Mineral Development

Mining employs 4000 Nova Scotians, about half of them in the coalfields, which produce about 2.2 million metric tons of coal a year. This fuel, which used to heat most Nova Scotian homes and factories, is now used mainly to generate electricity.

In 1978 the province depended on oil purchased from other countries for over two-thirds of its electrical generation. During the

Left: The oil rig *John Shaw* in Halifax Harbour. *Below*: The Windsor Salt Mine and loading facility in Pugwash

1980s the rising price of oil and uncertainty about supply led the province to convert its power stations to burn coal. By 1990, only 15 to 20 percent of the province's electricity was coming from imported oil. As the cost of electricity increases and concern for the environment grows, a renewed effort to encourage Nova Scotians to conserve energy has begun.

Gypsum, used for making wallboard and plaster, is mined in Hants and Victoria counties. Since the 1770s the mineral has been exported to the eastern and southern United States. The mining of salt at Pugwash began in 1957 and is a major source of employment in the town. North America's only tin mine lies near East Kemptville in Yarmouth County. It opened in 1986 and closed in 1992.

During the 1970s and 1980s many Nova Scotians hoped that the province might become a "have" province — that is, less dependent upon the federal government. The hope for a more prosperous future was based on the discovery of oil and gas near Sable Island. The dream of quick wealth from beneath the sea faded when the deposits proved to be too small. Oil production from offshore fields began in the 1990s, with small quantities being produced. Gas from deposits near Sable Island may be tapped for markets in Canada and the United States after the year 2000.

Manufacturing and Trade

Nova Scotia has only a few large manufacturing companies, but many small ones. The three Michelin tire plants employ over 3000 workers, about one-tenth of all manufacturing jobs. The market for textiles is small in Atlantic Canada, but several textile plants operating in Truro, Windsor and Bridgetown are exploring new markets and developing new products.

Industries using high technology have begun to establish themselves in the province in recent years. Pratt and Whitney makes aircraft engines outside Halifax and Nautel, in Hackett's Cove is one of the world's leaders in radio beacons. A number of "high-tech" companies apply research from government and university laboratories to produce electronic devices. A doctor in Halifax developed a software program that trains medical students to diagnose diseases. Nova Scotia is promoting itself as "Canada's Technology Playground." In 1992, Nova Knowledge came into being to bring together everyone interested in the development of information technology and knowledge-based industries.

Recently the Nova Scotia government has been encouraging local entrepreneurs in the creation of small businesses. Nova Scotia has had people like this in the past, and several one-person businesses turned into large companies.

In 1907 Frank Sobey's father opened a butcher's shop in Stellarton, Pictou County. His son turned it into a vast commercial empire

Fishing for lobsters, operating a computer and factory work are just a few of the hundreds of ways in which Nova Scotians today earn their living.

that now owns supermarkets, food wholesalers, drugstores and other ventures. Izaak Walton Killam had little formal education, but he became one of the richest men in Canada. Killam built his fortune on publishing, utilities, pulp and paper and other enterprises. The inheritance taxes from his estate provided $50 million to launch the Canada Council in 1957.

Other entrepreneurs were born outside Nova Scotia. Hector Jacques, from Goa in India, founded a consulting engineering company in 1972. It began with two employees. It now has 450. Ken Rowe came to Halifax from England in 1964 to work for a marine supply company. He started his own company which has sales of more than $300 million a year from marine, aerospace, aviation and other ventures including a jointly-owned hotel in Moscow.

About 90 percent of all businesses in Nova Scotia — some 32 000 ventures — employ fewer than fifty workers. Most of them serve local markets, but some have been very aggressive in making new products and finding new buyers for their goods. One Yarmouth company sells specially equipped ambulances to countries as far away as Turkey and Morocco. A Pictou firm produces high-quality knives that are sold all over the world. Another business in Kentville produces an extract to treat arthritis from evening primroses.

The co-operative and credit union movement which began in the 1930s remains strong. New Dawn began in Sydney, in 1973 by rescuing a local handicraft enterprise. Then it moved into house building. This community-owned venture, with assets worth over $10 million, operates dental clinics, group homes and services for seniors. Smaller co-operatives on the island do landscaping, cut timber and strive to keep alive the Gaelic language and culture.

Tourism

The provincial government has placed increasing emphasis on tourism as a way of creating employment and income. It promotes the

Left: Buskers come from around the world to perform at Halifax's Annual International Street Performers Festival. *Above*: Each spring Kentville celebrates the Annapolis Valley's apple industry with its Apple Blossom Festival and Parade.

restful atmosphere of Nova Scotia and its heritage and history. In 1995 more than a million tourists spent $925 million in the province. The industry employs about 30 000 people during a season lasting from mid-May to the end of October.

Nova Scotia describes itself as "Canada's Festival Province." Year round, visitors and residents come together at festivals, fairs, exhibitions, folk concerts and other special events. Windsor has the oldest agricultural fair in North America, dating from 1765. Lunenburg holds a fisheries exhibition every summer, while the Annapolis Valley Apple Blossom Festival celebrates the bounty of the land. Acadians recall their return to Nova Scotia in song and dance at Wedgeport, Grand Pré, Chéticamp and other communities.

Historic sites like Louisbourg and a number of restored homes show how Nova Scotians once lived. Many sea captains' houses have become inns where visitors can enjoy modern comforts while absorbing Nova Scotia's fascinating history.

CHAPTER 8
The Nova Scotia Lifestyle

In the days of wooden ships, the Halifax waterfront bustled with activity. The change to containers has left many of the old piers and docks unused. Now large parts of the waterfront are parking lots.

A popular Farmers' Market operates in the stone building near the waterfront that once housed Keith's Brewery. Here farmers sell herbs, flowers, plants and vegetables. Fish farmers offer fresh salmon caught the day before. Craftspeople display their work. City dwellers crowd the market, buying home-made cheese, sausages and bread, catching something of the spirit of the old days when Nova Scotians made everything they needed.

Nova Scotians are a cautious, conservative people, wary of change. Yet change is the only constant thing in life these days in the province. To many people in the rest of Canada, Nova Scotia is a place of fishing villages and quiet communities sleeping in the summer sun. This view may be based on books like Ernest Buckler's *The Mountain and the Valley* and Charles Bruce's *The Channel Shore*. But these writers also told how hard life was in Nova Scotia.

Many rural Nova Scotians still earn a living by fishing or cutting wood, but many also drive school buses, work on roads, process fish, and work in hundreds of other casual and seasonal jobs. Unemployment insurance helps tide many people over times when work is scarce. Obtaining a steady job is the goal of most young Nova Scotians. The economy makes this difficult.

Haligonians (as the residents of Halifax are called) celebrate their city's birthday with street parties, parades, concerts and a spectacular fireworks display.

Development versus the Environment

During the 1980s, the need for jobs and concern about the environment created conflict. In 1981 when uranium was found near Windsor, a local citizens' organization forced the government to ban uranium mining. Recently a plan to import hazardous waste for incineration on the South Shore was stopped because of concern about the effects on the environment. When the Nova Scotia Power Corporation proposed building a plant at Point Aconi in Cape Breton to generate electricity from locally mined coal, environmental organizations took the Corporation to court to stop construction. The plant would use new technology to reduce the effects of the heavy sulfur content of the coal, but the groups were still concerned that it would damage the environment by increasing greenhouse gases. The plant went ahead and came on stream in September 1993.

Many communities are caught between their need to create employment and the desire to maintain the environment and a pleasant lifestyle. Some towns such as Windsor, Mahone Bay and Bridgewater have become vigorous centres, attracting new businesses. Others, like Bridgetown, Digby and Glace Bay have been hard hit by the closing of factories and plants.

While the population of many towns in Nova Scotia has remained stable, there has been a slow drift of people from the countryside to the cities, in particular to the Halifax–Dartmouth area. About a third of Nova Scotians live in and around these two cities and their suburbs. People commute from towns in the Annapolis Valley and the South Shore to work in the twin cities.

Other kinds of change are affecting smaller communities. At one time every community had its own telephone system and power company. Now Maritime Tel and Tel is the sole provider of telephone service. In the 1980s many small communities also lost their post office, train station and railway service. In 1992, the provincially-owned Nova Scotia Power Corporation was sold to private investors.

The small South Shore fishing village of Prospect sits at the tip of a peninsula facing the Atlantic Ocean.

As economic life declines and jobs that used to exist disappear, poverty has become more visible — a number of communities have set up food banks. Even in relatively prosperous Halifax, homeless men and women beg for a handout. While life remains good for many people, it has become harder for those on the fringes of society to make a living.

Blacks and Native Peoples

For members of the black and native community, poor economic conditions have made life harder. Blacks and native people tend to suffer higher levels of unemployment or work in poorly paid jobs.

The ancestors of some black Nova Scotians fought for the British during the American War of Independence. When the Black Loyalists arrived in Canada they received small parcels of poor-quality land near white communities. After the War of 1812, black refugees settled on rocky, barren land near Halifax. In the 1840s their descendants moved to the shores of Bedford Basin and founded the community of Africville. It had a church and an elementary school by the end of the century. As Halifax grew, the city located an open dump near the community. The residents fought desperately to retain a sense of pride and identity, but the city saw Africville as a problem area. Between 1964 and 1967 the people were moved into public housing and their homes were bulldozed. This event left bitter memories among Nova Scotia blacks.

Many blacks also live in Preston, just outside Dartmouth, near the lakes that supply the city with water. In 1977, the city stopped them from building more houses because of possible pollution. This time leaders of the black community and government officials worked together. They drew up a plan that allowed the communities to grow while ensuring that Dartmouth had a clean water supply.

With the help of the Black Cultural Centre near Dartmouth, black Nova Scotians have begun to rediscover and recover their history. And they have found reason for pride by learning about their heroes and heroines. William Hall, a sailor from Hantsport, won the Victoria Cross (the British Empire's highest award for bravery) in 1857. Portia White, born in Africville, became a world-famous opera singer. Nova Scotia had the first black lawyer in Canada, Delos Davis of Sydney; and the first black policewoman, Rosa Fortune of Annapolis Royal. Black poets and playwrights like Maxine Tynes, Walter Borden and George Elliott Clarke give voice to the joys and sorrows of their people.

The native peoples of Nova Scotia are also learning about their past and preparing for the future. Rita Joe, a poet, and Noel Knockwood, a spiritual leader, celebrate the traditional way of life. At the

Micmac Friendship Centre in Halifax, young men and women learn to use computers.

About 14 000 Micmac live on and off the thirteen reserves in the province. High unemployment has led to community-based ventures to create jobs. Small manufacturing and service industries have started at Eskasoni, Whycocomagh and Membertou. Eskasoni has a locally elected school board. Here a native development corporation sees aquaculture and tourism as ways to generate jobs.

The fate of one young Micmac revealed the plight of members of minority groups in Nova Scotia. In 1971 the police arrested seventeen-year-old Donald Marshall, son of the Grand Chief of the Micmac Nation. Convicted of the murder of Sandy Seale, a black teenager, Marshall went to jail. He spent eleven years there before a review of his case proved his innocence.

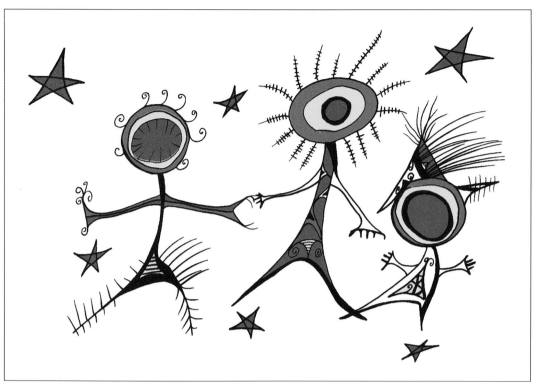

Family by Micmac artist Alan Syliboy. A mystical family floating along the Milky Way represents the pathway to heaven. The strength of the Micmac people originates in the family bond.

In 1988 the provincial government set up a royal commission to find out what had gone wrong. The Marshall Enquiry revealed serious problems with the legal system and discrimination against native peoples and blacks in Nova Scotia. In 1990 Dalhousie University started to train black and native lawyers.

The Acadians

Nova Scotia's original European settlers, the Acadians, have survived for almost 400 years. Today, there are about 40 000 people of Acadian descent in the province. They make up about a third of the population in Richmond, Digby and Yarmouth counties.

Among the most popular features at Acadian festivals held yearly in several communities are the demonstrations of traditional Acadian dances.

Until the 1970s, the French language was in danger of dying out, but a revival of Acadian culture has produced a renewed pride in Acadian heritage.

The Centre Acadien at Université Ste-Anne holds the largest collection of Acadian archives in the provinces. Many fishing companies on the French Shore and elsewhere are owned by Acadians. During the 1970s and 1980s many Acadians entered the professions and government. Acadian education has steadily improved. A Francophone school opened in Dartmouth in the late 1980s and Acadian areas have their own school boards. Cultural organizations and festivals help preserve Acadian traditions.

Managing the Tensions of Change

In the nineteenth century Nova Scotians looked outward to the world as they traded with other countries. Along the coasts of the province houses still face the sea. Over the past hundred years, with

A huge, colourful paper dragon is paraded through the streets of Dartmouth as part of the Chinese New Year celebrations.

a declining economy, many Nova Scotians turned in on themselves. They sought to hang on to what they had rather than take risks and try to start new ventures.

Although the province has never attracted large numbers of immigrants, about forty ethnic groups now live in the province. Roughly 1500 immigrants settle in Nova Scotia each year. It has often been the new people who have brought about change.

Dutch men and women who settled near Mabou and Antigonish have created flourishing farms. In the 1970s Americans fleeing the cities and military service came to Nova Scotia for the peace and quiet of a new life. Two Americans started a pewter and silversmithing venture in Pugwash. Its products are sold throughout

A meditation practice in the main shrine room of Karma Dzong
Buddhist Church in Halifax

the world and the company employs 300 people. Two other Americans bought a farm near Lunenburg and a cow named Daisy. When she produced more milk than they could drink, they began to make yogurt — and a new business came into being. Vietnamese immigrants have opened several restaurants in Halifax. And the city has become the headquarters of Tibetan Buddhism in North America.

These newcomers have brought fresh vitality to the province. At the political level, self-reliance, local initiative and co-operation are being seen as the keys to the future development of Nova Scotia. The premiers of Nova Scotia, New Brunswick and Prince Edward Island have met to discuss ways of working together more closely for the benefit of their provinces — and the region.

CHAPTER 9

Recreation, Sport and Culture

Clockwise from centre: Winter fun; the Nova Scotia International Tattoo; fishing dory races at Lunenburg; puppet show; *The Swimmer*, painting by Alex Colville; the Halifax Public Gardens

Nova Scotia licence plates describe the province as "Canada's Ocean Playground." The sea has always provided Nova Scotians with recreation. As early as 1826, sailing and rowing regattas were organized in Halifax by the military. Each summer, and well into the fall, white sails fill harbours, coves and inlets around the province. The Royal Nova Scotia Yacht Squadron was founded in 1837, seven years before any other yacht club in North America and twenty-five years before the first one in Great Britain.

Rowing remained popular until recently. George Brown of Herring Cove dominated the sport from 1864 until his death in 1875. He was champion oarsman of the world in 1874. Dartmouth hosted the World Junior Canoe Championships in July 1989, the first ever held outside Europe. One of the most popular events in Nova Scotia is war canoe racing; the canoes carry fourteen paddlers and a coxswain. All Nova Scotians have ready access to wilderness in two national and many provincial parks. Canoe routes take the traveller inland along some of the rivers used by the native peoples, and sea kayaking along the coast is becoming popular.

Some hardy people even enjoy winter surfing along beaches near Halifax.

Team Sports

Scottish immigrants to New Glasgow introduced the sport of curling to Nova Scotia in the 1820s. By the 1850s, regular bonspiels (tournaments) in the province brought curlers together to compete. A Nova Scotia team won the first Brier, the annual national bonspiel, in 1927.

Nova Scotians of all ages participate
enthusiastically in the many sporting activities
available to them.

Nova Scotia now has only one minor professional hockey team,
the Cape Breton Oilers in Sydney. It has also sent a number of stars
to the National Hockey League in recent years, including Bobby
Smith, Mike McPhee, Al MacInnis, Paul Boutilier and Paul
MacLean. Danny Gallivan, a Sydney native, became one of the best-
known voices in Canada, broadcasting games of the Montreal
Canadiens for thirty-two years.

Soccer has become increasingly popular in Nova Scotia in recent years.

While cricket is still played on the Halifax Commons in summer, baseball overtook it in popularity in the late nineteenth century. Now softball is more popular than baseball. Soccer has enjoyed a rising popularity, which, however, has not yet reached a level that will support a professional team. In the same way, basketball remains a popular amateur sport.

Some Nova Scotia Champions

Because of its small population, Nova Scotia has never been famous for big-time professional sport. But it has produced some outstanding athletes.

George Dixon, born in Africville in 1870, had his first professional fight at sixteen and became world bantam and featherweight champion. He once fought twenty-two bouts in a week, but died penniless in 1906. A community centre in Halifax's North End bears his name. Sam Langford, born in Weymouth in 1883, has been rated

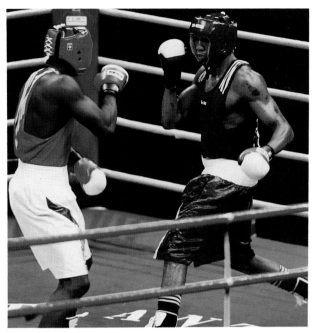

Left: David Defiagbon (right) on his way to winning a silver medal at the 1996 Summer Olympic Games. *Above:* George Dixon of Halifax is still considered one of the great boxers of all time.

the seventh-greatest heavyweight boxer of all time by one of the sport's top writers. At the 1996 Summer Olympics, David Defiagbon won a silver medal in the heavyweight (91 kg/200 lbs) division in boxing.

Track and field events began in 1850 when the British troops in Halifax organized the first Garrison Games. One of Nova Scotia's most famous runners was Johnny Miles, who won the Boston Marathon in 1926 and 1929. A marathon named after him has been run every year since 1975 in New Glasgow. Aileen Meagher, another amateur runner, won an Olympic bronze for Canada at the 1936 Berlin Games and five British Empire medals.

In February 1981, the late Robert McCall of Dartmouth became the first Maritimer ever to win a gold medal in the Canadian Figure Skating Championships. He and his partner Tracy Wilson went on to win a bronze medal at the Winter Olympics in 1988, the first-ever Olympic dance medal for Canada. The pair also won the bronze at the World Figure Skating Championships in 1986, 1987 and 1988.

The Craft Heritage

Nova Scotia has a vast range of cultural activities, and has always been especially strong in crafts.

Micmac people used porcupine quills for the decoration of their clothing and goods. During the nineteenth century they became skilled woodworkers and basket makers. With just a knife and a plane an Acadian could build his own house, barn and furniture. Woodworking skills flourished in the days of sail. Nova Scotians knew how to carve everything from keels to figureheads.

European settlers brought traditional designs and patterns to their new home — and thrifty habits. Discarded clothing became rugs, quilts and coverlets. Quilting brought women together to contribute their individual skills to a collective work. On Cape Breton, men and women on isolated farms spun locally grown wool and wove coverlets, place mats and blankets. People came together for spinning bees and for milling frolics where they sang as they stretched and softened the cloth.

The old craft heritage almost died out during the Second World War. However, when Mary Black became head of craft development for the provincial government in 1943, she helped revive the crafts tradition. Quality of work and the ability to make simple and useful things became the mark of Nova Scotia crafts.

In the 1970s, many newcomers turned to crafts to make a living. By 1993, 300 craft businesses employed more than 3000 people and generated sales of over $30 million. One example is that of Vicky Lynn Crowe who came home from the United States in 1972 and began making quilts, using small brightly coloured pieces of cloth called suttles. New Germany in Lunenburg County is the home of her company, Suttles and Seawinds, which now produces clothing as well as quilts and other household items.

In 1991, the provincial government opened the Nova Scotia Centre for Craft and Design in downtown Halifax. The gallery there is named after Mary Black.

Left: Craft store owners at Mount Uniacke display a fine example of local hand work. *Below:* A potter attracts a fascinated audience at the Annapolis Royal Craft Market.

Cultural Connections

The great upsurge of cultural activities in recent years has not only created jobs and improved incomes. It has strengthened the sense of pride in Nova Scotia's achievements, locally and provincially. In culture, Nova Scotia is as rich as any other part of Canada.

The history of the Art Gallery of Nova Scotia illustrates the rising interest in the arts in the province. It began in 1975 as a room in the wall of the Halifax Citadel. It now occupies a handsome restored Victorian building near the waterfront. The nearby Nova Scotia College of Art and Design, founded in 1887 by Anna Leonowens, holds its classes in the stores and offices once used by Halifax's merchants.

Canada's first feature film was produced in the province. In 1913 the Canadian Bioscope Company of Halifax used Henry Wadsworth Longfellow's poem *Evangeline*, the tragic tale of lovers

The cast of the TV news parody show *This Hour Has 22 Minutes* (left to right): Mary Walsh, Greg Thomey, Cathy Jones and Rick Mercer. This award-winning series is written and produced in Halifax.

separated during the Acadian deportation, as the basis for a movie of the same name. The movie was a success, but the company went out of existence in 1915. Interest in filmmaking rose in the 1980s, and by 1991 the province had forty-nine film production companies in operation. The National Film Board's Atlantic regional office in Halifax has provided valuable training for young filmmakers.

There has always been strong support for Symphony Nova Scotia and Neptune Theatre in Halifax. Dance, theatre, heritage events, craft fairs, multicultural celebrations, choirs, artists and writers flourish in every corner of the province. Many communities have built centres for cultural events. In Pictou the specially designed DeCoste Entertainment Centre hosts activities ranging from Shakespeare plays to pop groups. Mermaid, a puppet theatre, has toured the world from its base in Windsor. The Mulgrave Road Co-operative Theatre operates from Guysborough, using co-operative methods to create works on local issues.

Nova Scotia is home to many artists. Alex Colville lives in Wolfville. His painting of a black horse rushing towards a railway train has become one of the best known in Canada. Tom Forrestall, an-

Rita MacNeil at the Big Pond Concert, held annually in her hometown of Big Pond, on the east shore of Bras d'Or Lake

other "magic realist" painter, lives in Dartmouth. And the province is rich in writers. Hugh MacLennan, author of *Two Solitudes* and *Barometer Rising* (set in the Halifax Explosion), grew up in Glace Bay. Thomas Raddall, one of Canada's foremost historical novelists, set many of his books in his home province. Ernest Buckler and Charles Bruce described life in small communities. The changes taking place in the province have served as a source of inspiration for Alastair MacLeod, Silver Donald Cameron, Harry Bruce, Bill Percy, Joyce Barkhouse, Budge Wilson, Harry Thurston, Susan Kerslake and others.

Nova Scotia has a strong musical tradition, especially in Cape Breton, where singers, pipers, fiddlers, step dancers and highland dancers perform at open-air Scottish concerts in many communities. Rita MacNeil lives at Big Pond on Cape Breton and has become famous for her heart-felt songs about the lives of working people.

As cultural activities in all fields have expanded in Nova Scotia, the province's rich heritage of folk art has gained increased recognition. The Micmac and early settlers delighted in making beautiful and useful objects. The names of these first artists have often been lost. But their work remains to tell of their dedication and skills, showing that creativity and a concern for beauty are deeply rooted in the history of Nova Scotia.

CHAPTER 10
Around the Province

Nova Scotia's landscape is dominated by seascapes. Its long coastline provides an amazing variety of views and experiences. Let's start where most of the people live.

The Halifax-Dartmouth Area

Halifax lies on a peninsula between its ice-free harbour and the North West Arm. The tall office buildings which rise behind the city's waterfront proclaim its role as the main commercial and business centre of Atlantic Canada. The city has seven degree-granting institutions — more than any other city in Canada — making it the region's educational centre.

Across the harbour lies the city of Dartmouth. Its industrial parks contain many of the province's service and small manufacturing industries.

Both cities have renovated their waterfronts. Alderney Gate, near the Dartmouth ferry landing, is named after the ship that brought the first settlers to the city in 1750. It houses Dartmouth's main library. Across the harbour, at Historic Properties, stores and offices occupy buildings once owned by privateers and merchants. Two bridges span the harbour where it narrows at the entrance to Bedford Basin. Grey-painted vessels line the shores of the naval dockyard near the site of the Halifax explosion.

The Halifax Citadel dominates the city's downtown, offering a view over the harbour. Built in 1856, it is the fourth fortress on the

Overleaf: The famous lighthouse at Peggy's Cove, a small fishing village on the South Shore, and one of the most photographed spots in the Maritimes

Above: One of the two bridges that link the sister cities of Halifax and Dartmouth. *Right*: The Halifax Citadel was used as a military base until after the Second World War. It is now a National Historic Site.

site. Each summer the Citadel comes alive as soldiers go through their paces for tourists. The buildings recall the days when Halifax was a major British military base. Below the Citadel stands the Old Town Clock, a symbol of the city since 1803. Farther down the hill, City Hall faces St. Paul's Church, the oldest existing Anglican church in Canada, across the Grand Parade.

Halifax, a compact, walkable city of mainly wooden houses, has many heritage buildings and quiet tree-lined streets surrounding the downtown business district. The city's charm is enhanced by the oldest formal Victorian Gardens in North America. At the tip of the peninsula lies Point Pleasant Park, an oasis of peace and quiet.

The South Shore

The road west from Halifax to Yarmouth sweeps along the South Shore, past white sand beaches, coves, low headlands and houses bedecked with wooden butterflies. Tourists flock to Peggy's Cove, a small fishing village a short drive from Halifax, to catch a glimpse of a bygone time, watch the seas pound the shores and send post-cards from the only post office in Canada located in a lighthouse.

Each town on the South Shore has a unique setting. Chester, a yachting centre, attracts wealthy Canadian and American summer

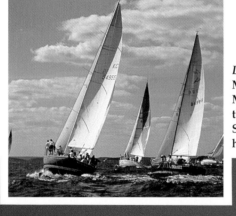

Left: Chester Race Week, held every August at Chester, on Mahone Bay, is the biggest sailing regatta in the Maritimes. *Below*: The town of Mahone Bay is famous for the three churches–Trinity United, St. John's Lutheran and St. James Anglican–that have stood side by side at the head of the harbour for over a hundred years.

residents. A ferry connects it with Big Tancook Island, famous for sauerkraut. The road into Mahone Bay passes three magnificent wooden churches. The town's name comes from *mahonnes*, French pirate ships that once frequented this coast. Legend has it that pirates buried treasure on nearby Oak Island. In 1795 hunters stumbled on a depression on the island. Digging down they found a shaft that flooded with water. Since then, six lives have been lost and millions of dollars spent probing the mystery of the "Money Pit."

Lunenburg, Nova Scotia's most important fishing port, sits on a rocky hill, its handsome wooden houses recalling a prosperous maritime past. Docked at the Fisheries Museum of the Atlantic on the waterfront are two former deep-sea fishing vessels and a rum-runner from the days of prohibition. An aquarium and many exhibits tell of the fishing industry's history. Modern trawlers dock at the nearby National Sea Products plant.

Bridgewater, the largest town on the South Shore, has a Michelin tire plant — and an international ox-pull contest every July. Liverpool, once a centre of privateering, now depends on a pulp and paper plant for its economic base.

Beyond Shelburne, fishing communities cling to a bleak and rocky coast. In 1987, a freighter landed 174 Sikh immigrants illegally near Charlesville. The local people fed them peanut butter and jelly sandwiches before seeing them on their way to a new life elsewhere in Canada.

Cape Sable Island is still a centre for boat building. North of Cape Sable lie eight Pubnico communities, the heart of Acadian settlement on this coast. The South Shore route ends at Yarmouth which has ferry links with the New England states.

The French Shore and the Annapolis Valley

From Yarmouth, the traveller passes along the French Shore. This stretch of road has been called the longest main street in Canada.

Acadians, returning home "on tiptoe and by the back door" settled here. Their neat, painted houses line the highway from Salmon River to Digby. Inland stretch forests at whose centre lies Kejimkujik National Park. Digby is the base of the famous Digby scallopers.

From Digby a ferry crosses the Bay of Fundy to Saint John, New Brunswick. Digby Neck leads to Brier Island, home of Joshua Slocum, first man to sail alone around the world. It offers opportunities for whale and bird watching. Upper Clements Theme Park overlooks the Annapolis Basin.

When Nova Scotians talk about "the Valley," they mean only one — the Annapolis Valley, the long stretch of fruitful land between Digby and Windsor. Approaching Annapolis Royal, the Annapolis River swings ever wider as the valley opens up; the Annapolis Tidal Power Project, the first in North America, dams the river. Annapolis Royal, with its historic garden, offers another

Whales can often be sighted during the summer in the waters around Brier Island, the westernmost point in Nova Scotia.

glimpse of the past. Nearby Fort Anne has been rebuilt, and across the basin lies Champlain's reconstructed *habitation* at Port Royal.

A new highway bypasses the string of towns that serve the people of the pleasant land between North and South mountains — Bridgetown, Lawrencetown ("Beautiful Trees, Dangerous Curves"), Middleton, Berwick, Kingston and Kentville. Tall elms line the streets of most valley towns. Orchards with colourful blossoms in the spring and heavy with fruit in the fall are everywhere. Beyond North Mountain small fishing communities line the Bay of Fundy.

At Grand Pré, probably the most famous Acadian settlement, a statue of Longfellow's heroine Evangeline stands in front of the church. A museum illustrates Acadian skills in building dykes and making the land fertile for farming. A short distance away, an iron cross on private land marks the actual deportation site.

The Head of Fundy

Windsor, 65 kilometres (40 miles) northwest of Halifax, was home to Thomas Chandler Haliburton, judge, historian, politician and writer. Haliburton created one of the most famous characters in Canadian literature. Sam Slick, the Yankee clockmaker, is celebrated with a festival in August.

Beyond the causeway at Windsor exposed red mud flats shine in the sun, disappearing under water and reappearing as the tides of Fundy rise and fall. In the distance Cape Blomidon, home of Glooscap, Great Spirit of the Micmac, stands sentinel at the mouth of the Minas Basin. Further east along the basin, the Shubenacadie Canal was completed in 1861 to connect the Bay of Fundy with Halifax harbour at Dartmouth. It was used for less than ten years — a victim of the coming of the railway.

The area around Parrsboro and Joggins attracts rock and gem hunters and those interested in fossils. Gemstones can be picked up along the shore, and Parrsboro hosts an Annual Rockhounds'

Left: The statue of Evangeline and the church at Grand Pré. *Right*: The blockhouse at Fort Edward in Windsor was built by the British in 1750.

Roundup each August. The Fundy Geological Museum at Parrsboro tells the story of this region's ancient past. Inland from Parrsboro is the old coal mining town of Springhill, the home of singer Anne Murray.

Mystery surrounds a locally built ship. In 1872 the *Mary Celeste* was discovered afloat and deserted in the Atlantic. She had been built as the *Amazon* at Spencers Island on the Parrsboro shore. No trace of her crew was ever found, and she has become one of the great mysteries of the sea.

Beyond Spencers Island the road leads north to Amherst. West of Amherst the Tantramar Marsh connects Nova Scotia with New Brunswick.

Along the Strait of Northumberland

Across the Chignecto Isthmus from Amherst lies Tidnish and the remains of a ship railway. If it had been completed, it would have eliminated the voyage around Nova Scotia by linking Northumberland Strait with the Bay of Fundy. But money for its construction ran out in 1891.

Known as the Sunshine Coast, the stretch of land opposite Prince Edward Island has the warmest waters north of the Carolinas. Local folklore tells of a phantom ship frequently seen in the Northumberland Strait. Pugwash, a salt-mining centre, hosts an annual Gathering of the Clans in July. Anna Swan, born at Tatamagouche, toured with Barnum and Bailey's circus — she stood 228 centimetres (7 feet 6 inches) tall.

The Pictou-New Glasgow area, one of the cradles of Scottish culture in Nova Scotia, is also an industrial centre. The Nova Scotia Museum of Industry celebrates the development of the area. The *Samson*, Canada's oldest steam engine, has found a home here.

The highway to Cape Breton leads through a valley to Antigonish. Here the visitor receives *Ciad Mile Failte* — "One Hundred Thousand Welcomes — the traditional Gaelic greeting. The welcome is repeated as you cross the Canso Causeway and reach Cape Breton Island.

Cape Breton Island

Cape Breton is a world apart. "Capers" or "Caybretoners," hospitable and friendly to strangers, have a strong sense of their own identity. Unemployment may be high on the island, but its people have never lost their belief in the value of their unique way of life.

A trip around the Cabot Trail is an introduction to the charms of the island. The trail starts near Baddeck and runs up the Margaree Valley. A Salmon Museum and the Museum of Cape Breton Heritage tell of the life in this quiet corner of the island. Chéticamp on the west coast, famous for its hooked rugs and co-operatives, is the most Acadian of all Nova Scotia's communities. The trail loops around the northern tip of the island through majestic scenery, then sweeps down the east coast over Cape Smoky. At Englishtown, on

Cape Breton Highlands National Park. It is not difficult to see why Alexander Graham Bell once wrote: "I have seen the Canadian Rockies, the Andes and the Highlands of Scotland. But for simple beauty, Cape Breton outrivals them all."

the shores of St. Ann's Bay, lived the Cape Breton Giant, Angus MacAskill. The community of St. Ann's, site of the Gaelic College of Celtic Arts and Crafts, hosts Scottish events each year.

Beinn Breagh ("beautiful mountain") overlooks Baddeck. Here in 1886, inventor Alexander Graham Bell spent a summer. He fell in love with the place and built a home on the mountain. Along with others he formed the Aerial Experiment Association, and on February 23, 1909, John McCurdy piloted the *Silver Dart* into the air above Baddeck Bay. He was the first British subject in the British Empire to fly a powered aircraft. A museum in Baddeck celebrates

Left: **At the north end of Bras d'Or Lake is the Great Bras d'Or, a narrow channel connecting the lake to the Atlantic Ocean.** *Above*: **Beinn Breagh, Alexander Graham Bell's summer home**

Bell's genius. He is buried with his wife, Mabel, who was an inventor and scientific researcher herself, on the mountain they loved.

Sydney, capital of Cape Breton, lies in the heart of an industrial area. At one time, coal was king here, and the mines employed thousands of men. DEVCO which runs the coal mines on the island has laid off hundreds of miners in its quest to become profitable.

Fortress Louisbourg, 35 kilometres (22 miles) east of Sydney comes alive each year as local people put on the costumes of its eighteenth century residents. Every detail of life in a French colonial outpost has been reproduced — except for the smell of drying fish!

A secondary road from Sydney swings down the east coast of the Bras d'Or lakes to St. Peter's. Here a canal connects the lake with the Atlantic Ocean. Beyond the canal lies Port Hawkesbury, once the site of a number of industries, most of which have now closed. A large pulp and paper mill, owned by a Swedish company, remains in operation.

The Eastern Shore

A winding road from the Canso Causeway takes the traveller along the shores of the Atlantic Ocean. At the tip of the Eastern Shore lies the town of Canso which has depended on the sea for over 400 years.

A little farther along the coast, is Sherbrooke, a community frozen in time. The old gold mining and lumbering town is now an outdoor museum. Gold originally drew people to this fog-shrouded coast after a moose hunter stumbled on a deposit at Tangier in 1858. In 1936, a fall of rock trapped three men in the Moose River Mine. The rescue attempts created international interest as J. Frank Willis of the Canadian Radio Broadcasting Commission covered the event in one of the first on the spot broadcasts. After ten days, two men emerged alive from the mine.

Below: **The restored general store at Sherbrooke Village.** *Right*: **The annual Clam Harbour sandcastle contest**

Tangier became famous as the home of the late Willy Krauch and his sons, whose smoked salmon, mackerel and eel sell around the world. At Jeddore-Oyster Pond, the Fisherman's Life Museum recalls the traditional life-style of fishing people. The simple cosy house offers a marked contrast to the hustle and bustle of life in Dartmouth and Halifax, a short distance to the west.

A tour of Nova Scotia shows its many landscapes and lifestyles, but above all it shows a land that has been a home — to the Micmac for centuries; more recently to the dispossessed of many countries. People in the province have known booms and busts, reaped the bounty of sea and land and learned to adapt to hard times and limited opportunities. Somehow they developed a life-style that offers a great deal of satisfaction to many people. They remain proud of their past and of what they have contributed to Canada.

Martinique Beach on the Eastern Shore is the longest beach in Nova Scotia, and one of the most beautiful.

Facts
at a Glance

General Information

Entered Confederation: July 1, 1867

Origin of name: Latin for New Scotland; first appears in the charter granted to Sir William Alexander by King James I in 1621.

Provincial Capital: Halifax, founded in 1749, incorporated as a city in 1841.

Provincial Nickname: "Canada's Ocean Playground." Nova Scotians call themselves "bluenosers." The name may have come from potatoes with a bluish tip once grown in the province. It could also refer to the blue-painted bows of small fishing boats, or to the dye that stuck to the noses of sailors when they rubbed them with home-knitted gloves.

Provincial Flag: Based on the arms granted to Sir William Alexander in 1625, the flag consists of the cross of St. Andrew, patron saint of Scotland. The cross is blue on a white background, the reverse of the flag of Scotland. In its centre is the red lion of Scotland on a gold shield.

Provincial Tartan: The first provincial tartan in Canada, it was registered in 1956. The colours are those of the provincial landscape and the Nova Scotia flag — blue, green, white, red and gold.

Provincial Motto: *Munit Haec et Altera Vincit* — "One defends and the other conquers."

Provincial Flower: Mayflower (trailing arbutus)

Provincial Tree: Red spruce

Provincial Gemstone: Agate

Provincial Mineral: Stilbite

Provincial Song: "Farewell to Nova Scotia." The origin of this song is unknown. It was popularized by folklorist Helen Creighton.

Population

Population: 938 205 (July 1995)

Population Distribution: Urban 57%; Rural 43%. However, many Nova Scotians live in unincorporated areas near cities and towns. Most of the population lives in coastal communities with few people inland.

Cities (1991)

Halifax	114 455
Dartmouth	67 798
Sydney	26 063

Towns (1991)

Glace Bay	19 501
Truro	11 683
Bedford	11 618
New Glasgow	9 905
Amherst	9 742
Yarmouth	7 781
New Waterford	7 695
Sydney Mines	7 551
North Sydney	7 260
Bridgewater	7 248
Kentville	5 506

Population Growth

Year	Population
1851	276 900
1871	387 800
1891	450 400
1911	492 300
1931	512 800
1941	578 000
1951	642 600
1961	737 000
1971	789 000
1981	847 400
1986	873 200
1991	899 942
1995	938 205

Geography

Borders: Connected to New Brunswick by the Chignecto Isthmus. The Bay of Fundy, Northumberland Strait and the Atlantic Ocean form its other borders.

Highest Point: White Hill, Cape Breton, 573 m (1880 ft.)

Lowest Point: Sea level

Distances: Northeast to southwest (Cape North to Cape Sable), 560 km (348 mi.). No part of the province lies more than 60 km (37 mi.) from the sea.

Area: 55 491 km² (21 420 sq. mi.); 3809 islands.

Rank in area among provinces: Ninth

Rivers: Principal rivers include the Annapolis, Cornwallis, La Have, Margaree, Mersey, Mira, Musquadoboit, St. Mary's and Shubenacadie. Most of the rivers are short, but their historical and economic significance cannot be overlooked. The Sackville and Shubenacadie rivers were used for early transportation by the Indians while today the Margaree and the St. Mary's are popular for salmon fishing. The Mersey is important to the lumber industry and others support hydroelectric power plants.

Lakes: Over 3000 lakes dot the landscape of Nova Scotia. The largest is Lake Bras d'Or occupying the centre of Cape Breton Island. On the peninsula, the largest is Lake Rossignol. Other large lakes are the Ainslie, Fishers, Gaspereau, Malaga, Sherbrooke and Shubenacadie.

Coasts: Nova Scotia has 7579 km (4710 mi.) of shoreline. The eastern and southern shores of the peninsula, on the Atlantic Ocean, are indented with hundreds of bays and coves. Many make fine harbours. The shores along the Northumberland Strait and the Bay of Fundy are straighter and good harbours are scarce. In Chignecto Bay and Minas Basin, part of the Bay of Fundy, the tides are the highest in the world. Their average daily range is about 10 m (35 ft.).

Islands: Nova Scotia is divided into two major parts — the peninsula itself and Cape Breton Island. There are more than 3800 smaller islands in the waters surrounding Nova Scotia. Many have interesting geographic features and folktales associated with them.

Bear Island at the mouth of the Bay of Fundy has rock "pillars" that extend hundreds of metres into the sea. According to legend, Oak Island is the site of Captain Kidd's hidden treasure. Five Islands at Minas Basin are supposed to be great clumps of earth thrown angrily by Glooscap, the legendary hero of the Micmac, at a mocking foe.

Topography: Most of southern Nova Scotia consists of rough, hilly upland. The highest land in this part of the peninsula is about 210 m (700 ft.). The area is made up of hard rock with many short rivers and lakes. There are some lowlands suitable for farming but most land is heavily forested.

Northern Nova Scotia is very different. The rocks are softer and the soil is good for farming. Some farm-

land has been reclaimed from the sea by dykes. Much of Cape Breton Island is a wild, hilly plateau rising to 573 m (1880 ft.) at White Hill, the highest point in the province. There are lowlands at the southern tip of the Island.

Climate: Cold air masses from the heart of Canada and warm air masses from the Atlantic Ocean influence Nova Scotia's weather. At times in winter it can be bitterly cold but usually Nova Scotia has a mild winter climate especially on the southern coast. Rain and snow are common. The summer climate is pleasantly warm and sunny with an average temperature of 24° C (74° F). Inland is usually warmer than along the coast.

The annual rainfall varies from about 1000 mm (40 in.) in the northern interior to 1400 mm (55 in.) in the south. Snowfall is usually about 175 cm (70 in.) in all areas. Fog often occurs along the south coast in the spring and summer when warm air passes over coastal waters. Ice sometimes blocks ports in the northern part of Nova Scotia and Cape Breton Island in winter, but the southern coast and Bay of Fundy are ice-free and remain open year-round.

Nature

Trees: Balsam fir, red spruce, pine, oak, maple, alder, tamarack, bog laurel

Wild Plants: Mayflower, wild iris, pitcher plant, white water lily. Edible

Starfish

Shellfish: Lobsters, mussels, oysters, scallops, clams

Sea Mammals: Harbour seal, grey seal, right whale, humpback whale

Connections and Communications

By Air: Regular flights connect Halifax to most Canadian cities as well as to Boston, New York and London, England.

By Sea: Ferries connect Yarmouth with Portland and Bar Harbor in Maine; Digby with Saint John in New Brunswick; Caribou with Wood Islands in Prince Edward Island; and North Sydney with Port-aux-Basques and Argentia in Newfoundland.

By Road: The Trans-Canada Highway crosses the Tantramar Marsh, passes through Truro, then heads east through Antigonish and across the Canso Causeway to North Sydney. The province's primary road network parallels the coastline throughout most of the province.

By Rail: Nova Scotia has only one passenger railway line. Via Rail runs from Halifax to Moncton via Truro and Amherst.

Newspapers: Nova Scotia's six daily papers are published in Amherst, Halifax, New Glasgow, Sydney and Truro. About thirty community newspapers are published in the province.

wild plants include crab apple, beach pea, blackberry, blueberry, burdock, cat tail, camomile, red clover, dandelion, fiddlehead, greenbriar, labrador tea, wild lettuce, pig weed, plantain, wild red raspberry, wild rose, wild strawberry, violet, winter cress

Animals: Moose, caribou, white-tailed deer, black bear, beaver, bobcat, chipmunk, otter, snowshoe hare, porcupine, skunk, marten, cougar, coyote

Birds: Blue jay, redstart, yellow goldfinch, black-capped chickadee, bald eagle, double-crested cormorant, great blue heron, starling, grackel, phalarope, shearwater

Fish: Cod, haddock, pollock, halibut, red fish, flounder, swordfish

TV and Radio: Most small towns have an FM and AM radio station and cable TV service. Halifax is the headquarters of CBC Radio and TV, and has a number of private radio and TV stations. Sydney has a CBC radio station and a private TV station.

Government

Federal: Nova Scotia has 11 members in the House of Commons and 10 appointees in the Senate.

Provincial: There are 52 members of the House of Assembly.

Local: Nova Scotia's three cities — Halifax, Dartmouth and Sydney — have been incorporated into regional municipalities. The Halifax Regional Municipality has a population of 330 000, the Cape Breton Regional Municipality has 120 000. In all, the province now has 55 municipal units. Some of the 39 towns have become part of the regional municipalities. There are more than 250 small communities.

Voting Qualifications: Canadian citizen or British subject, at least 18 years old, who has lived in the province for six months.

Economy, Industry and Employment

Principal Products

Agriculture: Dairy produce, apples and other fruit, poultry and eggs, hogs, cattle, hay, nursery plants

Manufacturing: Food products, rubber products, paper and allied products, transportation equipment, metal products, wood products, high-tech and marine-related goods, crafts, clothing

Natural Resources: Coal, gypsum, salt, lumber sand, gravel

Business and Trade: The head offices of several large national corporations are located in Nova Scotia, which also has 21 of the top 50 companies in Atlantic Canada. About 90 percent of all firms in the province have fewer than 20 employees. Nova Scotia accounts for 1.5 percent of manufacturing shipments in Canada, and for more than a third of those in Atlantic Canada. Much of the business growth in recent years has been in the service industries, which accounted for 73 percent of the province's output in 1993 and for 70 percent of the total employment. Nova Scotia has a total of about 30 000 small businesses.

The Balmoral Grist Mill near Tatamagouche

The Fisheries: In 1995, Nova Scotia had 7400 registered fishermen and 5850 workers in processing plants, a drop of over 2000 since 1990. The number of people involved in aquaculture, however, continues to rise totalling 386 in 1995. The value of fish products exported also continues to rise as processing plants import fish from elsewhere in the world. New species such as snow crab are now being caught. The commercial fishing of salmon has been discontinued, but the sports fishery continues and is worth $1-2 million to the province.

Employment and Income: Nova Scotians earn 75 percent of their income from employment and 15 percent from transfer payments. Per capita incomes in Nova Scotia in 1994 were $18 916, just over 80% of the Canadian average, with family incomes totalling $46 524. About 33% of Nova Scotians were involved in administration and management, with another 41% in clerical, sales and service occupations. Primary occupations accounted for just under 6% of the labour force, with processing, construction and transportation employing about 20% of workers. Unemployment averaged 12.1% in 1995 and was higher in Cape Breton.

Education

Nova Scotia has 12 degree-granting institutions, including the Nova Scotia Agricultural College. Seven of the other institutions including the Atlantic School of Theology, the Technical University of Nova Scotia and the Nova Scotia College of Art and Design are located in Halifax. The Nova Scotia College of Geographical Sciences is located in Lawrencetown. The province has 14 community colleges. The new *Collège d'Acadie* operates from six locations to serve the Acadian population through distant education methods. The Atlantic Provinces Special Education Authority operates Resource Centres for the Visually and Hearing Impaired in Halifax.

In 1995-96, Nova Scotia had 164 020 students in grades primary to 12 in 471 schools. About a third of all students go to schools in the Halifax Regional Municipality. The Department of Education also lists 33 private schools in the province.

Social and Cultural Life

Museums: Practically every community in Nova Scotia has a local museum. The federal government, through Parks Canada, runs 16 National Historic Sites and Parks. The Nova Scotia Museum operates 25 provincial sites and museums. Rising interest in the province's heritage has led to the placement of plaques on significant old properties. In 1995, the village of Maitland became the province's first Heritage Conservation District. In 1996, the town of Lunenburg was designated a United Nations World Heritage Site.

Libraries: The Provincial Library, established in 1952, coordinates eleven regional libraries across the province. Bookmobiles travel to areas that do not have regular branches. Additional libraries are provided by the universities as well as by government research centres such as the Bedford Institute of Oceanography in Dartmouth.

Music: Scottish settlers have given Nova Scotia, and particularly Cape Breton Island, its unique heritage of Gaelic singing, highland dancing and bagpipe playing. The Gaelic College at St. Ann's and St. Francis Xavier University at Antigonish both sponsor summer festivals, plays and musicals. Symphony Nova Scotia performs throughout the province, with a regular season in Halifax.

Sports and Recreation: Nova Scotia has one minor-professional hockey team, the Cape Breton Oilers in Sydney. Cricket, soccer, softball, baseball and watersports including windsurfing, sailing and swimming are popular during the summer months while curling, skating and tobogganing flourish in the wintertime.

Over a million people visit Nova Scotia during the summer. They, as well as the residents, are attracted by the beautiful scenery, numerous historical sites and the opportunity for fishing, hunting, hiking and other recreational activities. The provincial government operates 95 day-use parks and 19 camping sites. Because the sea is always close by, Nova Scotia is described as "Canada's Atlantic Playground."

National Historic Parks

Fort Edward, at Windsor, was built by the British in 1750; it served as a centre for the deportation of the Acadians.

Grand Pré is located near the site where 2000 Acadians were deported in 1755; a bronze statue of Longfellow's heroine Evangeline stands before a church of Norman design — from one side she appears to be a young girl, from the other side, an old woman.

Fort Anne at Annapolis Royal offers a lovely view over the Annapolis Basin, which it once guarded.

Port Royal faces Fort Anne on the other shore of the Annapolis Basin. The *habitation* has been reconstructed from original descriptions and drawings to show how the first settlers lived.

Kejimkujik National Park lies in southwestern Nova Scotia, in a landscape of gently rolling hills, lakes and rivers. It has a number of hiking and canoe routes and is open year-round.

Fort Anne National Historic Park, Annapolis Royal

Halifax Waterfront Buildings bring the world of nineteenth-century Halifax alive. *Bluenose II* docks here during the summer, and a pleasant walk links the area to the ferry terminal.

Halifax Citadel looms over Halifax. Built in a star-shape, the citadel served as the centre for British regiments but never heard a shot fired in anger. Barrack rooms have been restored and an Army museum forms part of the complex.

Louisbourg has risen from its ruins through an ambitious restoration project. About one-fifth of the fortifications and the town has been rebuilt. Guides in period costume tell of life in the summer of 1744, and food prepared in the manner of the time is available.

Alexander Graham Bell National Historic Park at Baddeck, Cape Breton, illustrates the many aspects of this famous inventor's genius.

St. Peter's Canal was completed in 1869 at St. Peter's, a centre for the fishing industry in Cape Breton.

Cape Breton Highlands National Park covers most of the northern tip of the island. The Cabot Trail, a modern, paved 303-km (188-mi.) highway runs along three sides of the park. A number of interpretation centres offer an introduction to the natural history of the area.

Marconi National Historic Site, Glace Bay, marks the site where Guglielmo Marconi transmitted the first "wireless" message across the Atlantic on December 15, 1902.

Other Interesting Places to Visit

Museum Headquarters near the Halifax Public Gardens offers special delights and programs to children as well as being the best place to start to learn about the history, geography and life of Nova Scotia.

The Maritime Museum of the Atlantic on the Halifax waterfront tells the story of Nova Scotians and the sea. Its exhibits include photographs and artifacts from the Halifax Explosion. Visitors catch the smell of rope and tar in the reconstructed ship chandler's store.

Ross Farm Museum at New Ross traces the history of agriculture in the province from 1603 to 1907. The farm is geared to the needs of young people seeking to learn about life on the land.

The Fisheries Museum of the Atlantic in Lunenburg tells the history of Nova Scotians who went to sea to fish. Two vessels at the dock show the conditions under which men and boys served at sea.

The Wile Carding Mill in Bridgewater, built in 1860, is the last of its kind in the area where once seven such mills operated.

The Perkins House, built in 1766, belonged to Simeon Perkins a merchant, shipowner and privateer who kept a diary of his life and times.

The Ross-Thomson House in Shelburne is the original store established by George and Robert Ross to meet the needs of the Loyalists who flocked here in 1783-84. Nearby, the *Dory Shop* recalls the small, well-built boats once so important in Atlantic Canada.

The Barrington Woolen Mill, begun as a community enterprise in 1882, has a unique collection of machines for spinning wool. *The Barrington Meeting House* once formed the focus of life for 50 families from Cape Cod who settled here in 1765.

The Firefighters Museum in Yarmouth contains examples of almost every type of fire engine ever used in the province.

North Hills Museum, a small wooden dwelling at Granville Ferry, houses fine examples of old furniture, porcelain and glass.

The Haliburton House in Windsor, built in 1836, was the home of Thomas Chandler Haliburton, creator of Sam Slick, *The Old Clockmaker*. Also in Windsor is the ornate *Shand House* with lots of gingerbread trim.

Uniacke House in Mount Uniacke was the magnificent home of Sir Richard John Uniacke. Built in 1813-15, it offers a glimpse of the life among the wealthy of the time.

Lawrence House at Maitland was built around 1870 by William Lawrence. It overlooks the shipyard where the owner's "Great Ship," the *William D. Lawrence* was launched.

Balmoral Grist Mill near Tatamagouche offers visitors a glimpse of how wheat, oats, barley, rye and buckwheat were made into flour in the last century.

The Sutherland Steam Mill in Denmark marks the time when water gave way to steam as a source of power. The mill cut lumber for Britain during the Second World War and produced the gingerbread trim seen on many local houses.

Fisherman's Life Museum at Jeddore-Oyster Pond recalls the simple, self-sufficient life of coastal dwellers that persisted until very recently.

Sherbrooke Village contains 25 restored buildings that date from the era of lumbering and shipbuilding.

Cossit House, the oldest house in Sydney, was built in 1787. It has been restored to the way it looked when it was occupied by its first owner, Rev. Ranna Cossit, the first Anglican minister in Cape Breton.

Significant Dates

1497 John Cabot lands on coast of North America, exact site unknown

1605 First European settlement at Port Royal

1613 Samuel Argall attacks and burns Port Royal

1621 James I grants Nova Scotia to Sir William Alexander

1632 Acadia is returned to France

1654 Port Royal is captured by the English

1667 Treaty of Breda restores Acadia to France

1713 Treaty of Utrecht gives Acadia back to England (but not Cape Breton or Prince Edward Island)

1745 Louisbourg taken by the New Englanders under command of Sir William Pepperell

1749 Halifax founded by Col. Edward Cornwallis

1750 The *Alderney* brings first settlers to Dartmouth

1751 Bartholomew Green, Jr. establishes Canada's first printing press in Halifax

1753 The "Foreign Protestants" arrive in Lunenburg

1755 Deportation of the Acadians

1758 First Representative Assembly meets at Halifax Court House; Louisbourg besieged and taken by British troops

1759 First settlement at Truro

1764 Windsor founded

The famous Lighthouse at Peggy's Cove

1773	The *Hector*, carrying Scottish immigrants, arrives at Pictou
1783	Loyalists arrive in Shelburne
1784	Nova Scotia and New Brunswick separated into two colonies; Cape Breton becomes a separate colony
1820	Cape Breton rejoined to Nova Scotia
1840	The *Britannia*, the first Cunarder, arrives in Halifax
1843	Dalhousie College formally opened
1848	Nova Scotia becomes first British colony to secure responsible government
1864	Free School Act introduced
1867	Nova Scotia enters Confederation
1879	Act creates 18 counties in Nova Scotia
1901	Steel mill begins operations at Sydney
1902	First official transatlantic message sent by Marconi from Glace Bay to Cornwall
1906	Britain relinquishes the last of her military bases in Canada, at Halifax
1909	First controlled flight in heavier than air machine in the British Empire at Baddeck
1917	Halifax explosion
1918	Women's suffrage legislation receives Royal Assent in Nova Scotia
1921	Schooner *Bluenose* launched at Lunenburg
1925	Five-month strike in Cape Breton mines
1936	Moose River Mine disaster
1958	Seventy-four men die in Springhill mining disaster
1967	Nova Scotia government buys Dominion Steel and Coal Co.
1970	Oil tanker *Arrow* goes aground in Strait of Canso
1975	Art Gallery of Nova Scotia opens in Halifax Citadel
1979	Oil tanker *Kurdistan* breaks apart in Cabot Strait
1984	North America's first tidal power plant begins operation at Annapolis Royal
1992	An underground explosion at the Westray mine in Pictou County kills 26 workers
1995	Grand Pré proclaimed Rural Historic District
1996	Act passed to establish Nova Scotia Arts Council

In June 1995, Saint George's Round Church, built in Halifax in 1800, was damaged by fire. Phase I of a $6 million restoration was completed in November 1995, when a reproduction of the dome and cupola was lifted into place.

Alexander Graham Bell

Sir Robert Borden

John Cabot

Andrew R. Cobb

Important People

Robert Morris Aitken (1939-), born in Kentville; flutist, composer; has gained renown as a soloist with orchestras in Europe, North America and Asia; his own music is highly original and includes electronic and oriental techniques

Henry Alline (1748-1784), moved to Nova Scotia where he was ordained in 1779; he created a religious revival known as the "New Light" movement; a prolific writer and persuasive preacher, he was a major influence on the establishment of the Baptist Church in the Maritimes

Alexander Graham Bell (1847-1922), the inventor of the telephone, built his summer home in Baddeck. He formed the Aerial Experiment Association with **John Alexander Douglas McCurdy** (1886-1961), **Frederick Walker (Casey) Baldwin** (1882-1948) and two Americans; their *Silver Dart* made the first manned flight in Canada in 1909; their Hydrofoil *HD-4*, is preserved in the Bell Museum at Baddeck

William Richard Bird (1891-1984), born in East Middleton; writer; served in the First World War and produced one of the finest books ever written on the ordinary soldier's view of war, *Ghosts Have Warm Hands*; his

two most popular novels, *Here Stays Good Yorkshire* and *Judgement Glen* won the Ryerson fiction award

Sir Robert Laird Borden (1854-1937), born at Grand Pré; lawyer, politician, prime minister from 1911 to 1920; gave strong leadership during the First World War; in his later years he was recognized as an international statesman, and was a firm advocate of the League of Nations

John Cabot (c.1449-1498), navigator, explorer; in May 1497 he landed on the shores of North America in Labrador, Newfoundland or Cape Breton Island, claiming the lands for England; many people believe Aspy Bay on Cape Breton Island to have been the location of his landfall; a cairn marks the spot

Rt. Rev. Moses Michael Coady (1882-1959), born in North West Margaree; priest, educator; first director of the Extension Department at St. Francis Xavier University; co-founder of what is known as the Antigonish Movement the growth of which is chronicled in his book *Masters of Their Own Destiny*

Andrew Randall Cobb (1876-1943), architect, established his practice in Halifax in 1912 and designed many of the city's major buildings

Enos Collins (1774-1871), born in Liverpool; privateer, merchant; bought the *Liverpool Packet*, with which he made a fortune from captured booty during the War of 1812; was reputed to be the wealthiest man in the Lower Provinces

Edward Cornwallis (1712-1776), was appointed governor of Nova Scotia after serving 17 years in the army; he arrived in 1749 with about 2500 English settlers to found the town of Chebucto, later renamed Halifax; he returned to England in 1752

Helen Mary Creighton (1899-1989), born in Dartmouth; folklorist, song collector; starting in 1928, with her primitive recording equipment on a wheelbarrow, she travelled around Nova Scotia, collecting traditional songs and stories; published many collections of songs and folk tales, including *Bluenose Ghosts* and *Bluenose Magic*, and an autobiography, *My Life in Folklore*

Samuel Cunard (1797-1865), born in Halifax; founded the British and North American Royal Mail Packet Company in 1839 and won the British government contract to carry mail to Canada and the United States; in 1878 the company became the Cunard Steamship Company, which dominated the Atlantic passenger trade

Sir John William Dawson (1820-1899), born in Pictou; geologist, principal of McGill University; first Canadian-born scientist to gain a worldwide reputation; founded Royal Society of Canada. His son **George Mercer Dawson** (1849-1901), was also a geologist who won many honours; his geological explorations in the Yukon Territory led to the naming of Dawson City in his honour

Joseph Frederick Wallet Des-Barres (1722-1824) military engineer, surveyor, governor; employed by the British Admiralty in 1763 to prepare charts of the coastline and offshore waters of Nova Scotia; in 1784, he was appointed the first lieutenant-governor of Cape Breton

Cyrus Stephen Eaton (1883-1979), born in Pugwash; one of America's great industrialists and financiers; in the hope of improving international relations, he founded the Pugwash Conferences which brought together scientists and other leading figures from East and West

Abraham Gesner (1797-1864), born near Cornwallis; geologist, chemist and inventor; in 1853 perfected a lamp oil that he called kerosene; also developed asphalt paving; has been called the founder of the modern petroleum industry

Edward Cornwallis

Helen Creighton

Cyrus Eaton

Abraham Gesner

Thomas C. Haliburton

William Hall

Joseph Howe

Anna Leonowens

John Howard Gray (1946-   ), playwright; grew up in Truro; his best-known play, *Billy Bishop Goes To War*, a controversial portrait of Canada's famous First World War flying ace, won the Governor General's Award for Drama in 1983

Thomas Chandler Haliburton (1796-1865), born in Windsor; author, judge, politician; served in the House of Assembly; appointed to Nova Scotia Supreme Court in 1841; his best-known work, *The Clockmaker; or the Sayings and Doings of Sam Slick*, brought him an international reputation; among the sayings Haliburton coined are "raining cats and dogs," "barking up the wrong tree," "facts are stranger than fiction"

William Hall (1838-1904), son of a black slave brought to Nova Scotia from Virginia during the War of 1812; he won the Victoria Cross for his bravery while serving in India in 1857; he was the third recipient of the VC, the British Empire's highest award for valour

Joseph Howe (1804-1873), born in Halifax; journalist, politician, premier and lieutenant-governor; mainly as a result of his efforts, Nova Scotia acquired responsible government in 1848; served as premier (1860-63); between 1866 and 1868 led the movement against Confederation; entered the federal cabinet in 1869; was appointed lieutenant-governor of Nova Scotia in 1873 but served only three weeks before his death

Rita Joe (1935-   ), born in Eskasoni; community helper, poet; her poems reflect a pride in her cultural heritage and close observation of the people around her; she is one of a group of Micmacs who are writing stories in Micmac to be read to children in Indian communities

Izaak Walton Killam (1885-1955), born in Yarmouth; built up an investment empire in Canada and Latin America; many institutions benefited from Killam money, including the Canada Council and the Izaak Walton Killam Hospital for Children in Halifax

Anna Leonowens (1834-1915), lived in Halifax from 1876 to 1897; her books about her experiences as a governess at the court of the King of Siam became the basis of the musical *The King and I*; among her many activities in Halifax was the founding of the Nova Scotia College of Art and Design

Thomas McCulloch (1776-1843), born in Scotland and came to Nova Scotia in 1803; became one of the Maritimes' finest teachers and theologians; founded Pictou Academy in 1816 and became first president of Dalhousie University in 1838

Angus Lewis Macdonald (1890-1954), born at Dunvegan; lawyer and politician; became premier in 1933; served in the federal wartime cabinet as minister of defence for naval services; returned to Nova Scotia in 1945 and served as premier until his death

James B. McLachlan (1869-1937), labour leader; born in Scotland and immigrated to Cape Breton in 1902; led coal miners during the bitter strikes of 1909 and the 1920s; became a newspaper editor and continued to fight for decent wages and conditions until his death

Hugh MacLennan (1907-1990), born in Glace Bay; novelist and professor; his first novel, *Barometer Rising* (1941), was set in Halifax at the time of the explosion; three of his novels — *Two Solitudes* (1945), *The Precipice* (1948) and *The Watch that Ends the Night* (1959) — won the Governor General's Award

Rita MacNeil (1944-   ), born in Big Pond; entertainer; has become one of Canada's most popular singers; attracted national attention in the early 1980s with her moving songs of working men and women; has toured internationally

Robert Breckenbridge Ware MacNeil (1931-   ), of the *MacNeil-Lehrer Newshour* on public broadcasting in the United States since 1983; grew up in Halifax; has published his autobiography, *Wordstruck,* and a novel, *Burden of Desire*

Aaron Roland Mosher (1881-1959), born in Halifax County; trade unionist; served as first president of the Canadian Brotherhood of Railway Employees; in 1927 became president of the newly formed All-Canadian Congress of Labour, a position he retained when it was succeeded in 1940 by the Canadian Congress of Labour

Anne Murray (1945-   ), born in Springhill; pop singer; her recording of "Snowbird" in 1969 won a Gold Record for her in 1970, her first of several; has received both Juno and Grammy awards; was made a Companion of the Order of Canada in 1985; in 1990, a museum housing Anne Murray memorabilia opened in Springhill

Thomas Head Raddall (1903-1994), writer; came to Nova Scotia in 1918; won three Governor General's Awards: in 1943 for his collection of short stories, *The Pied Piper of Dipper Creek and Other Tales;* in 1948 for his history of the provincial capital, *Halifax, Warden of the North;* and in 1957 for *Path of Destiny;* best known for his historical novels, especially *His Majesty's Yankees* and *The Governor's Lady*

Angus Macdonald

James B. McLachlan

Robert MacNeil

Anne Murray

Robert Stanfield

Maxine Tynes

Sir Richard Uniacke

Sir John Wentworth

Joshua Slocum (1844-1909), born in Wilmot Township; sailor, author; went to sea at 16; in 1893 rebuilt a derelict sloop, the *Spray*, in order to sail around the world; his book *Sailing Alone Around the World* is a classic of seafaring literature

Clarence Eugene ("Hank") Snow (1914-   ), born in Liverpool; country and western singer-songwriter; his most famous song, "I'm Moving On," established his career in the United States in 1950, and in 1985 won the Millionaire Award for having been played one million times on the radio, an all-time country music record

Robert Lorne Stanfield (1914-   ), born in Truro; lawyer and politician; considered one of Nova Scotia's outstanding premiers; rebuilt an almost extinct provincial Conservative party, becoming leader in 1948; served as premier from 1956 to 1967 then switched to federal politics and became leader of national Conservative party; resigned from politics in 1976

Sir John Sparrow David Thompson (1845-1894), born in Halifax; lawyer, politician, judge and prime minister; became member of legislative assembly in 1877 and served as attorney general from 1878-82; switched to federal politics in 1885 and served as justice minister and as prime minister from 1892 to 1894

Rev. James John Tompkins (1870-1953), born in Margaree; priest, educator; from 1906 to 1922 he was vice-president of St. Francis Xavier University; co-founder of the Antigonish Movement

Sir Charles Tupper (1821-1915), born in Amherst; doctor, politician, diplomat, prime minister; entered politics in 1855 and became premier in 1864; supported Confederation and in 1867 became a Member of Parliament and served as minister of several portfolios; was prime minister for ten weeks in 1896

Maxine N. Tynes (1949-   ), teacher, writer, poet and freelance broadcaster; traces her heritage back to the Black Loyalists; graduate of Dalhousie University, was the first Black Nova Scotian to sit on its Board of Directors; lives and teaches in Dartmouth

Sir Richard John Uniacke (1753-1830), lawyer, politician; came to Nova Scotia from Ireland in 1774; appointed solicitor general in 1781 and attorney general in 1797. His son **Richard John Uniacke** (1789-1834) was a member of the Cape Breton Legislative Council and chief justice of Cape Breton; later he represented Cape Breton County in the Nova Scotia assembly; became a judge of the Supreme Court of Nova Scotia in 1830. Another son, **James Boyle**

Uniacke (1800-1858) became the first premier of Nova Scotia after the winning of responsible government in 1848

Sir John Wentworth (1737-1820), Loyalist, governor; appointed governor of Nova Scotia 1792; he was personally popular but the second half of his governorship (the longest in the province's history) was marked by constant conflict with the Assembly

Portia White (1910-1968), born in Truro; classical singer; the internationally known contralto performed across Canada and Central America and in New York; at the height of her career she was known as the "Marion Anderson of Canada"

Sir William Young (1799-1887) served as premier from 1854 to 1860, when he resigned to become chief justice of Nova Scotia; noted later in life for his philanthropy

Portia White

Premiers of Nova Scotia Since Confederation

Hiram Blanchard	Liberal	1867
William Annand	Anti-Confederation	1867-75
Philip Carteret Hill	Liberal	1875-78
Simon Hugh Holmes	Conservative	1878-82
John S. D. Thompson	Conservative	1882
William T. Pipes	Liberal	1882-84
William S. Fielding	Liberal	1884-96
George H. Murray	Liberal	1896-1923
Ernest H. Armstrong	Liberal	1923-25
Edgar N. Rhodes	Conservative	1925-30
Gordon S. Harrington	Conservative	1930-33
Angus L. Macdonald	Liberal	1933-40
Alexander S. MacMillan	Liberal	1940-45
Angus L. MacDonald	Liberal	1945-54
Harold J. Connolly	Liberal	1954
Henry D. Hicks	Liberal	1954-56
Robert L. Stanfield	Conservative	1956-67
George I. Smith	Conservative	1967-70
Gerald A. Regan	Liberal	1970-78
John M. Buchanan	Conservative	1978-90
Roger Bacon	Conservative	1990-91
Donald Cameron	Conservative	1991-93
John Savage	Liberal	1993-

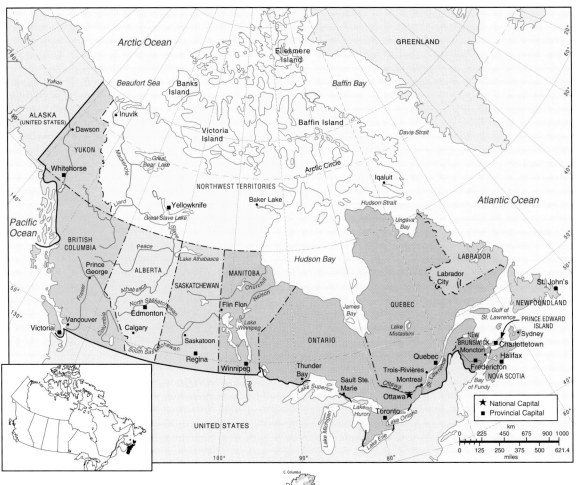

Arctic Ocean

GREENLAND

Ellesmere
Island

Beaufort Sea
Banks
Island

Baffin Bay

Yukon

ALASKA
(UNITED STATES)

Dawson

Inuvik

Victoria
Island

Baffin Island

Davis Strait

YUKON

Mackenzie

Great
Bear Lake

Arctic Circle

Whitehorse

Iqaluit

Pacific
Ocean

Liard

Yellowknife

Baker Lake

Hudson Strait

Atlantic Ocean

NORTHWEST TERRITORIES

Great Slave Lake

Ungava
Bay

BRITISH
COLUMBIA

Peace

Slave

LABRADOR

Prince
George

Lake Athabasca

Fraser

ALBERTA

Athabasca

North Saskatchewan

Edmonton

Calgary

SASKATCHEWAN

MANITOBA

Churchill

Nelson

Hudson Bay

Labrador
City

St. John's

NEWFOUNDLAND

Columbia

Flin Flon

James
Bay

QUEBEC

Gulf of
St. Lawrence

PRINCE EDWARD
ISLAND

Lake
Mistassini

Victoria

Vancouver

Saskatoon

South Saskatchewan

Lake
Winnipeg

NEW
BRUNSWICK

Sydney

Charlottetown

Regina

ONTARIO

Moncton

Halifax

Winnipeg

St. Lawrence

Fredericton

NOVA SCOTIA

Red

Thunder
Bay

Trois-Rivières

Bay
of Fundy

Sault Ste.
Marie

Montreal

Lake Superior

Ottawa

Ottawa

★ National Capital

UNITED STATES

Lake
Huron

Lake Michigan

Toronto

Lake Ontario

Lake Erie

■ Provincial Capital

km
0   225   450   675   900 1000

miles
0   125   250   375   500 621.4

Topography

0   200   400 MI.

0   200   400 KM.

© Hammond Inc., Maplewood, N.J.

5,000 m. | 2,000 m. | 1,000 m. | 500 m. | 200 m. | 100 m. | Sea | Below
16,404 ft. | 6,562 ft. | 3,281 ft. | 1,640 ft. | 656 ft. | 328 ft. | Level |

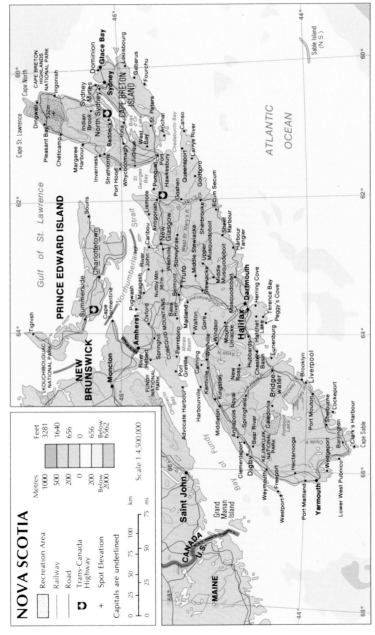

NOVA SCOTIA

Recreation Area

Metres	Feet
1000	3281
500	1640
200	656
0	0
200	656
Below 2000	Below 6562

— Railway

— Road

Ⓒ Trans-Canada Highway

+ Spot Elevation

Capitals are underlined

km
0 25 50 75 100
0   25   50   75 mi

Scale 1:4,500,000

© Rand McNally.

PRINCE EDWARD ISLAND

Gulf of St. Lawrence

NEW BRUNSWICK

ATLANTIC OCEAN

CANADA
U.S.

MAINE

Saint John

Moncton

KOUCHIBOUGUAC NATIONAL PARK

Tignish

Summerside

Charlottetown

Souris

Cape Tormentine

Northumberland Strait

Amherst

River Hébert

Springhill

COBEQUID MOUNTAINS

Oxford

Pugwash

Malagash

Nuttby Mtn. 367m

Tatamagouche

Bass River

Belmont

Truro

Stewiacke

Middle Stewiacke

Upper Musquodoboit

Middle Musquodoboit

Musquodoboit

Dartmouth

Halifax

Mount Uniacke

Windsor

Hatchet Lake

Terence Bay

Peggy's Cove

Herring Cove

Hubbards

Chester Basin

Lunenburg

Bridgewater

Brooklyn

Liverpool

Port Mouton

Shelburne

Lockeport

Clark's Harbour

Cape Sable

Barrington

Clyde R.

Wedgeport

Lower West Pubnico

Yarmouth

Port Maitland

Westport

Weymouth

Freeport

Hectanooga

KEJIMKUJIK NATIONAL PARK

Ponhook Lake

Caledonia

Bear River

Springfield

Clementsport

Digby

Annapolis Royal

Bridgetown

Middleton

Kingston

Kentville

New Ross

Gore

Walton

Maitland

Canning

Port Greville

Parrsboro

Advocate Harbour

Harbourville

Bay of Fundy

FUNDY NATIONAL PARK

Chignecto Bay

Minas Basin

Avon R.

Mersey R.

Medway R.

Grand Manan Island

Cape St. Lawrence

Cape North

CAPE BRETON HIGHLANDS NATIONAL PARK

Ingonish

Dingwall

Pleasant Bay

532m

Chéticamp

Margaree Harbour

Inverness

Port Hood

Strathlorne

Whycocomagh

St. Georges Bay

Mabou

Indian Brook

Sydney Mines

North Sydney

Baddeck

Iona

Bras d'Or Lake

Judique

West Bay

St. Peters

Arichat

Chedabucto Bay

Dominion

Sydney

Glace Bay

Louisbourg

Gabarus

Fourchu

CAPE BRETON ISLAND

Port Hawkesbury

Ponquet

Mulgrave

Goshen

Queensport

Canso

Larrys River

Goldboro

Ecum Secum

Sheet Harbour

Harbour

Tangier

Sherbrooke

Antigonish

New Glasgow

Stellarton

Westville

Caribou

River John

Pictou

West St. Mary's R.

St. Mary's R.

Musquodoboit

Lismore

Sable Island (N.S.)

AVERAGE ANNUAL RAINFALL

Nova Scotia's rainfall is heaviest along the eastern coast.

Mm		Inches
750-1,000	1	30-40
1,000-1,250	2	40-50
1,250-1,500	3	50-60

Figures within areas are for identification purposes only.

GROWING SEASON

The southern coast of Nova Scotia has more than five frost-free months a year.

Average Number of Days
in Frost-Free Period

1	80-100
2	100-120
3	120-140
4	140-160
5	160-180

Figures within areas are for
identification purposes only.

ECONOMY AND AGRICULTURE

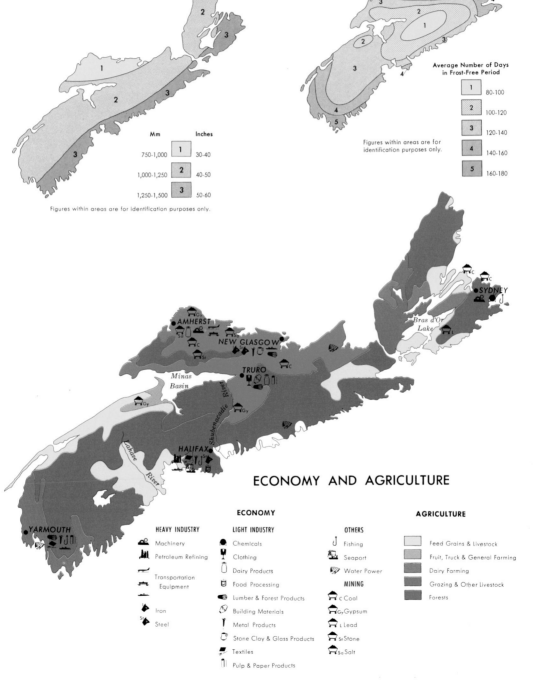

ECONOMY

HEAVY INDUSTRY
- Machinery
- Petroleum Refining
- Transportation Equipment
- Iron
- St Steel

LIGHT INDUSTRY
- Chemicals
- Clothing
- Dairy Products
- Food Processing
- Lumber & Forest Products
- Building Materials
- Metal Products
- Stone Clay & Glass Products
- Textiles
- Pulp & Paper Products

OTHERS
- Fishing
- Seaport
- Water Power

MINING
- C Coal
- Gy Gypsum
- L Lead
- Sr Stone
- Sa Salt

AGRICULTURE
- Feed Grains & Livestock
- Fruit, Truck & General Farming
- Dairy Farming
- Grazing & Other Livestock
- Forests

Index

About the Author

Jim Lotz was born in Liverpool, England. After graduating from university, he worked for a year in Nigeria then immigrated to Canada. He worked for the federal government, taught in various universities and eventually established himself in Halifax as a writer and consultant. During the seventies and eighties, he published a dozen books on Canadian history, including *Cape Breton Island*, *Prime Ministers of Canada*, and *Railways of Canada*.

Picture Acknowledgments

Front cover, © D. Humphreys/**The Stock Market Inc.**, **Toronto**; 2–3, 13 (right), 15 (background), 70, 103, © S. Swan/**The Stock Market Inc.**, **Toronto**; 4, 6, © T. Wegg/**The Stock Market Inc.**, **Toronto**; 5, 17, 34 (background), 40 (bottom), 50, 63, (right), 64 (left and right), 67 (bottom left), 75 (right), 80 (top left and centre), 81 (top left), 83 (top and middle), 87 (left), 90–91, 98 (left), 101 (right), 102 (left), 119 (middle bottom), 120 (middle top), © **Albert Lee** , **Halifax**; 8–9, 11, 22, 32, 69 (left), 76, 77, 80 (bottom left), 87 (right), 89, 94 (top), 96, 100, 102 (right), 112, **Nova Scotia Department of Tourism and Culture**; 13 (left), back cover, © Pierre St-Laurent/**The Stock Market Inc.**, **Toronto**; 14, 55, 59, **Nova Scotia Information Services**, 15 (inset), 108, **Bill Ivy**; 18, **Nova Scotia Department of Education, Education Media Services**; 21, 52, 116 (top), **Metropolitan Toronto Reference Library**; 24, **Nova Scotia Museum**; 25, **Environment Canada, Canadian Parks Service/Lewis Parker**; 26 (left), 57, 69 (right), 109, © Jessie Parker/**First Light**; 26 (right), **The Stock Market Inc.**, **Toronto**; 27, **Environment Canada, Canadian Parks Service/Dusan Kadlec**; 29 (bottom/PA938 and top/PA168), 39 (top/PA105692 and bottom/PA115381), 44 (PA41121), 54 (left/C698 and right/PA27012), 57 (inset/PA31002), 116 (middle top/PA27012), 117 (top/C11070), 118 (top/C6087 and middle bottom/C22002), 119 (bottom/PA164966), **Public Archives of Canada**; 30, **Confederation Life**, **Toronto**; 31, © Michael Philip Manheim/**First Light**; 34 (inset), **Courtesy of the Library of Congress, Washington, D.C. and the Bell family**; 35, **Courtesy of the Maritime Museum of the Atlantic, Halifax/Harold Lister Collection**; 37, **Courtesy of the Maritime Museum of the Atlantic, Halifax**; 40 (top), 60, © Janet F. Dwyer/**First Light**; 23, 41, 63 (left), 65 (top and bottom), 67 (top), 98 (right), © J. G. Dill/**Sky Photographic Services, Pugwash**; 42, **Art Gallery of Ontario, Toronto/Courtesy of the estate of Lawren P. Harris**; 46 (left), *The Halifax Herald*; 46 (right), 75 (left), 85 (right), 116 (bottom), 117 (middle top, middle bottom and bottom), 118 (middle top and bottom), 119 (top and middle top), 120 (top, middle bottom and bottom), 121, **Public Archives of Nova Scotia**; 48, **Beeton Institute, College of Cape Breton**, 67 (bottom right), **Nova Scotia Department of Industry, Trade and Technology**; 73 © Derek Trask/**The Stock Market Inc.**, **Toronto**; 76, **Alan Siliboy**; 78, **Multicultual Association of Nova Scotia**; 79, © **Marvin Moore Photography, Halifax**; 81 (top right), **Art Gallery of Ontario, Toronto/Courtesy of Alex Colville**; 81 (bottom right), © A. Schofield/**The Stock Market Inc.**, **Toronto**; 83 (bottom), **Tourism Halifax**; 84, **Bill Jensen, Halifax**; 85 (left) F. Scott Grant/**Canadian Olympic Association**; 88, **Salter Films International Ltd.**; 93 (top), **The Stock Market Inc.**, **Toronto**; 93 (bottom), © Lorraine C. Parow/**First Light**; 94 (bottom), © G. McGowan/**The Stock Market Inc.**, **Toronto**; 101 (left), Mia & Klaus/**Superstock**; 104 (background), **Forestry Canada**; 109, 114, © Tom Kitchin/**First Light**; 115, **Basil Grogono**.

97   45